The Third Generation Lotuses

Colin Chapman, the flying enthusiast, with his Piper, suitably registered G-PRIX (the other aeroplane was registered G-TEAM!), and a Lotus Esprit S2.

The Third Generation Lotuses

A collector's guide
by Graham Robson

MOTOR RACING PUBLICATIONS LTD
28 Devonshire Road, Chiswick, London W4 2HD, England

ISBN 0 900549 82 3
First published 1983

Photosetting by Zee Creative Ltd., London SW16
Printed in Great Britain by The Garden City Press Ltd.,
Letchworth, Hertfordshire

Contents

Foreword

by Mike Kimberley
Managing Director, Lotus Cars Limited

It is very pleasing to be able to enjoy reading a book which not only covers its subject very comprehensively, but also records events and achievements accurately. This *Collector's Guide* covering the Lotus products of the recent years has, I know, been deeply researched and contains a large amount of information concerning Lotus, not only productwise, but also as a company.

For those who know Lotus and knew the mercurial genius who founded the company, Colin Chapman (who inspired everyone he met and worked with to achieve normally impossible objectives), it will be realized that Lotus was built by a devoted, totally committed team of executives and staff and stands apart from the normal motor industry by virtue not only of its wealth of creative talent and innovative design (which is second to none in the industry), but also in respect of the intense loyalty and support given to the company by the whole staff.

Following the tragic premature death of Colin Chapman in December 1982, the year during which the company's fortunes were at a low ebb, due mainly to the non-existence of the USA market combined with the most massive worldwide recession ever experienced since motor cars were originally conceived, the ability of Lotus to respond quickly to changing circumstances has been demonstrated by the successful achievement of profitable trading during the first half of 1983.

This situation, coupled with the restructuring of our company to provide a sound and broad equity base for the future, will, I am convinced, result in Lotus achieving the world prominence and status it deserves. The company's current profile, which encompasses the most prestigious high-performance sports cars ever designed and built in the world, has been broadened by the development of a very high technology engineering consultancy business, which carries out work for a wide range of international clients, not only in the motor and commercial vehicle industry, but also in many other industries where advanced Lotus technology is desirable and can provide considerable product advancement.

This strengthening of the high-technology aspects of Lotus will, in conjunction with the creativity and abilities of its staff, position Lotus very favourably in the highly competitive and fast accelerating future motor industry.

The worldwide challenges of the future will be very demanding, with commercial performance depending even more heavily upon the excellence of the product in all respects. Lotus is ideally positioned to achieve the essential objectives of providing a high-quality and performance-exclusive product to the discerning owner, based upon its very advanced and creative high-technology base.

In a world where mass-produced cars will be the norm from a decreasing number of major international companies, the opportunities will increase for Lotus to provide a selective and outstandingly prestigeous product in limited numbers for the individual.

Introduction

I believe that this is the first book to concentrate exclusively on the modern generation of 16-valve-engined Lotus road cars, which have now been in production for a decade. It was high time that such a book was prepared, not because the cars were about to be dropped (which most certainly is not the case), but because there has already been a great deal of change in what has always been a fairly complex range.

But how should we describe these cars collectively in order to produce a title for the book which is easily understood? 'Elite, Eclat, Esprit, Excel' is accurate, but somewhat cumbersome for a main title, and the description 'E-models' is ruled out because, of course, earlier Lotus cars have also carried names beginning with the letter 'E'. Similarly, the term 'modern generation' had to be avoided because it would have become obsolete immediately the forthcoming Toyota-engined Lotus arrived on the scene.

In the end, the most logical title seemed to be *THE THIRD GENERATION LOTUSES*, even though it presupposes a certain historical expertise on the part of the reader in recalling that the original Elite represented the first and the Elan/Europa family the second generation of series-production Lotus road cars. We hope you agree!

My own judgment is that the cars covered in this book have been the making, and nearly the breaking, of the Lotus marque. They were brave in concept and advanced in engineering, but their specification was so up-market that sales were bound to be limited. Yet, when Colin Chapman conceived them in the late 1960s, he could not possibly have guessed that two severe oil price shocks and one major recession lay ahead in the 1970s.

Commercially, therefore, the new cars were always something of a gamble, and were sure to be costly to put into production, but this did not deter Lotus from forging ahead. Frankly, since the first of these new models, the Elite, appeared in 1974, Lotus' financial performance has been rather like the curate's egg — only good in parts. Nevertheless, it is to the everlasting credit of the cars themselves, the engineers who designed them, and the management team which never lost faith, that Lotus is still with us, that the cars have now established a reputation as 'classics', and that the future looks as bright and promising as it ever has been.

I fell in love with Lotus in 1957, after travelling to Earls Court to see the sensational new Elite — and fell out of love again as soon as I drove one of those cars! Throughout the 1960s I had flirtations with a whole variety of Lotus road cars, but somehow I never felt I actually needed to own one of them.

I'd better confess, here and now, that I have never owned one of the 16-valve-engined Lotuses (mainly because I am not what Mike Kimberley calls an entrepreneur to whom 'the difference between £14,000 and £16,000 is not all that significant'!), though I have driven all of them often enough to know that here I have found 'my' sort of car. I will always be grateful to my publisher, John Blunsden, for encouraging me to work out my Walter Mitty-like fantasies again, this time in print.

Although the number of these cars built so far (no more than 7,000 in all, by mid-1983) is small, interest in them is vast, and for that reason I hope that this *Collector's Guide* will be a help to all those who are already owning, or hoping to own, one of the cars.

Incidentally, in case anyone believes that this book was only written because the 16-valve-engined variety of Lotus was about to die, I can correct them straight away. There will certainly be a new type of Lotus from Hethel in the fairly near future, but it will be an additional range, rather than a replacement. I have every possible reason to hope and believe that the third-generation cars will continue for some years to come, and that one day this book will have to be updated.

GRAHAM ROBSON

Acknowledgements

In assembling material for this book, I often had to call on the Lotus factory and staff for assistance. Accordingly, I would like to thank Managing Director Mike Kimberley, not only for finding the time to be interviewed, but for allowing me to disrupt the smooth running of parts of the business at times, and letting me nag him into searching through the Lotus archive for historic material. Don McLauchlan, the company's Publicity Manager, not only dug out facts and figures which I needed, and opened doors which might otherwise have remained closed to me, but he provided a copious photographic store for me to raid. He also put me in touch with Sid Harper and Hugh Wilson, for more facts and figures.

Almost all the photographs come from Lotus' own archive, and from Focalpoint, of Norwich, so capably and cheerfully run by Ron and Brenda Middleton.

For corroborative facts on the Lotus tie-up with Talbot, my thanks go to Colin Cook of the Talbot Motor Company Ltd, for help on American comment regarding Lotus to the National Motor Museum Reference Library, and to Jeremy Walton, for his original research on Esprit matters.

As ever, I am grateful to *Autocar*, its Editor, Ray Hutton, and his assistants, including Warren Allport and Margaret Wentworth, and to *Thoroughbred & Classic Cars*, Editor Tony Dron, and his deputy Lionel Burrell, not only for being the best magazines of record, but for allowing me to quote from their back numbers, as I also acknowledge *Motor* (and Editor Tony Curtis) for further information.

Lastly, of course, I salute Lotus-watchers, all round the world, not only for their interest in the marque, but for the way they encourage Lotus to be more advanced and more inventive with every new model which appears.

GRAHAM ROBSON

The Elite of 1957 was Lotus' first true road car. Like every Lotus which followed it, it was sleek and purposeful, with an aerodynamically smooth body. The first Elite was a very light car, featuring monocoque glass-fibre construction, and styling was originally inspired by Peter Kirwan-Taylor. On this model the door glasses did not retract into the doors.

CHAPTER 1

Ancestors and heritage

Mk 1 to Europa

The story of Lotus is well known — but still remarkable. In essence, it is the story of one man's genius and enterprise, and it covers the evolution of a famous marque through trials specials, kit cars, racing sports cars, Grand Prix machinery and a series of exciting road cars. The first Lotus was built in 1947, the first sold to a customer in 1953, and the company has grown more famous with every succeeding year.

There is no space in this book to relate the many Lotus racing successes, except to point out that without the racing the company itself might not have become as well known, and that without the technical stimulus of racing the road cars might not have become as advanced. I ought to make it clear, by the way, that the connection between Lotus Cars and Team Lotus has been very tenuous indeed for many years — this being a fact of financial and commercial life which the Group Lotus annual report always spells out with care.

In broad terms, one could say that there have been four different families of Lotus road car, though in the context of this book I propose to dismiss the amazing Lotus Seven as a racing sports car which could be used on the road (Dennis Ortenburger, Lotus Seven authority, will understand, I hope). The first civilized Lotus road car, therefore, was the original Elite coupe of 1957-63, while the next complete family was the Elan/Plus 2/Europa series of 1962-75.

Colin Chapman had started supplying Lotus 6 kit cars in 1953 from a stable in Tottenham Lane, Hornsey, North London. His company had been founded with the aid of a £25 loan from his girl-friend Hazel (who subsequently became his wife) and at this time he was still a salaried employee of the British Oxygen

Company. He had already started to race his own products with some success, and his rise to fame was so rapid that for 1956 he was commissioned to design a new chassis space-frame for the Vanwall Grand Prix car. In 1957 he introduced his first Lotus single-seater (the Type 12 Coventry Climax-engined Formula 2 car), but in the same year he launched the original Elite.

Strictly speaking, the Type 14 Lotus, which became the Elite, was conceived with an eye to new Grand Touring car race regulations for 1,300cc cars, which explains why it was laid out more with an eye to function than to refinement and comfort. During 1957, it was Colin Chapman who designed the unique glass-fibre monocoque type of construction, and elected to use a single-cam Coventry Climax engine, while it was his accountant friend Peter Kirwan-Taylor, and Ron Frayling, who set about styling the car.

It is now well known that the Elite made its first public appearance before it had even been completed, let alone driven and developed, that it did not actually get into production until the end of 1958, and that it proved far too expensive to manufacture. Between 1958 and 1963, a total of 1,030 body/chassis units were built at a new Lotus factory in Cheshunt, a few miles further north, on the outskirts of London; it is generally agreed that nearly 1,000 of these were built up as complete (or complete kit) cars.

However, although the Elite was well-loved, usually from a distance by people who could not afford to buy one for themselves, it was not a commercial success. No less an authority than Colin Chapman was once quoted on this:

'The Elite was really a road-going race car, and used many of

The first Lotus road car to use a backbone chassis-frame was the Elan of 1962, and a lengthened version of this design was used for the Elan Plus 2 of 1967. The frame illustrated is that of the Plus 2. The principles of this frame have been retained into the 1980s.

the racing components. We didn't have much experience of road-going economics when we designed it, and without long-range tooling, long-range buying and strict cost-saving it was finally just uneconomic to build. I believe we lost over £100 on each car we built. Something had to be done, and so we started work on the Elan.'

The Elan was almost everything that the Elite was not — it was a convertible where the Elite had been a coupe, it had a separate chassis, it had Lotus' own brand of engine, it was refined and habitable and, above all, it was profitable. It helped Lotus forge strong links with Ford, links which they retained into the 1970s, and it represented a big step along the road to respectability as manufacturers, rather than as mere assemblers.

The two most important features in the definitive Elan were its separate, pressed-steel, backbone chassis-frame, and its Lotus-Ford twin overhead camshaft engine. The concept of the backbone frame, once adopted for Lotus road cars, has never been abandoned, while the engine programme was merely the first step towards making Lotus independent of engine supplies from any other concern.

In the beginning, it seems, there had been thoughts about building the Elan in unit-construction form, but as it was destined to be an open sports car in its original form this scheme was speedily dropped. As refined for series production, there was a backbone frame, in pressed steel, bifurcated at the front to pass at each side of the front-mounted engine and gearbox assembly, and supporting steel 'towers' to pick up the combined coil spring/damper units at the rear. The glass-fibre bodyshell, which had neat and simple styling, influenced once again by Peter Kirwan-Taylor, featured flip-up headlamps in the front wings, had Ford bumpers neatly moulded into the front contours, and was treated to the luxury of wind-up windows in the doors. (The original Elite window had to be removed if ventilation was needed!)

The famous twin-overhead-camshaft engine came into existence as a result of a typically complicated Chapman deal, whereby Ford would supply 1.5-litre five-bearing Cortina cylinder blocks and many other components, including the crankshafts, connecting rods and pistons, Lotus would design their own twin-cam conversion for the unit and J. A. Prestwich (JAP) of North London would machine it for them.

The engine design and conversion was the work of Harry Mundy, then *Autocar's* Technical Editor, already famous for his work at BRM and Coventry Climax (including designing the FPF

The original Elan was an open sports two-seater — and this is Michael Bowler, long-time distinguished Editor of *Thoroughbred & Classic Cars,* sampling a 1964 example.

Grand Prix engine along with Walter Hassan) and later to take charge of Jaguar's engine design team in the 1970s. The story goes that he had originally been commissioned to design an engine for Facel Vega, who then promptly ran out of money, and that the bare bones of his layout were revised and adopted for the Ford-Lotus application. Part of his brief was that the original Ford pistons were to be retained, which circumscribed the twin-cam valve gear somewhat, though he managed to keep the included valve angle down to 54 degrees. The top-end was classic twin-cam, which is to say that it had two valves per cylinder and a part-spherical combustion chamber. Right from the start the 1.5-litre engine produced 100bhp in road-going form, but later

racing units produced up to 180bhp with 1.8 litres and fuel injection.

(The story goes that Colin Chapman offered Mundy either a flat fee of £200 for doing the job, or a royalty of £1 per engine produced. Mundy, the realist, took the £200 — and regretted it ever afterwards. When Lotus built the 25,000th Lotus-Ford engine at the beginning of the 1970s and presented it to Ford with due ceremony, Mundy jokingly approached Chapman and offered to change his mind . . . Colin's reply was predictable!)

Although the Elan pre-dated the 1970s-variety of Elite by 12 years, its layout had several important pointers for the future. Firstly, of course, it had the backbone chassis, all-independent

11

After the open version, Lotus produced the Elan Coupe, a very civilized, if small, 'saloon' car. This was the S4 version, which had centre-lock steel disc wheels. Like the open model, many of these machines were sold as kit-cars to save the customer having to pay Purchase Tax.

The Elan Plus 2 was a definitive move up-market, for the wheelbase was 12in longer than that of the Elan, the tracks 7in wider, and there were two extra 'occasional' rear seats. The basic chassis layout, all-independent rear suspension and twin-cam engine were all retained. Lotus only sold the Plus 2 as a closed car . . .

. . . but Hexagon, one of their dealers, promoted this drophead conversion at one stage.

suspension by coil springs, and disc brakes at front and rear. It used a glass-fibre body — eventually available in open or coupe form — and it featured proprietary items like a Ford gearbox and a Ford differential, though in a special Lotus casing. There were other proprietary components (instruments, tail-lamps, switches and many other details) all round the car, but over the next few years most of these would be replaced by special Lotus-designed items.

At this point I should mention the Lotus-Cortina project. Even though it was a very important car at Cheshunt in terms of numbers built, it was not truly a Lotus, but more a 'homologation special' built for Ford. At first it was a very specialized version of the Ford Cortina GT, complete with Lotus twin-cam engine, close-ratio gears, coil spring rear suspension and light-alloy body panels, but by 1965 it had been transformed into simply a twin-cam-engined Cortina GT with standard bodywork and suspension. Lotus built these cars from 1963 to 1966, but the Mk 2 Lotus-Cortina which followed was to be built by Ford themselves, at Dagenham.

The Elan was a great success for Lotus in all respects except for that of reliability, and it could be supplied either as a built-up car, or as a near-complete kit. The kit-car concept was purely British in origin, and had come about because of a quirk in UK Purchase Tax laws. If a car was supplied complete, Purchase Tax had to be paid on the factory basic price, but if it was supplied as a kit and assembled by the owner and unpaid friends in a private garage, it came tax-free. There were all sorts of reasons why such procedures could be abused (they were . . . frequently), but there was no doubt that this appealed to many enthusiasts. Until the beginning of the 1970s, the supply of Lotus kit cars was a dominant part of the company's business.

Next, at the end of 1966, came the Lotus Europa (or Europe as it was known in, of all places, Europe), which was another example of Chapman astuteness and co-operation with another manufacturer. Although the Europa was different from the Elan in almost every detail at first, it was still recognizably of the same design philosophy, even though it had a mid-engined configuration, and power and transmission by Renault. The Europa, in fact, used a different type of backbone frame to which the glass-fibre bodyshell was permanently bonded at first, and the

There was enough room in the rear seats of the Elan Plus 2 for small, or young teenage, children, but if the front seats were pushed all the way back on their slides knee-room virtually disappeared.

1.5-litre Renault engine was an 82bhp unit adapted from that used in the front-wheel-drive Renault 16 hatchback.

In the meantime, other great things had been happening at Lotus. Not only had Jim Clark won two Formula 1 World Championships driving Lotus cars (in 1963 and 1965), but demand for the production cars had risen so much that the Cheshunt factory (which had been brand new in 1959) was bursting at the seams, and there was no further scope for expansion. After a brisk search, Lotus found an ideal new site at Hethel airfield, near Wymondham, a few miles south-west of Norwich. Not only was planning permission secured to build a new factory, but the airfield (an ex-USAF bomber base from the Second World War) had a ready made runway and perimeter

tracks, which would provide an excellent test track for the cars, and a landing strip for the Chairman's private aeroplane. As originally conceived, the factory was to have a 151,000sq ft single-storey production area and 26,000sq ft of ultra-modern open-plan offices and design facilities.

The target date for completion was originally set for October 1966, but there were some delays. An elegant but simple foundation stone in the office entrance now tells its own story:

'Laid, on the 17th of July 1966, by Colin Chapman, Founder.'

The move to Hethel, in fact, took place at the end of 1966, and in a very short time indeed Lotus had not only installed the production lines for their Elan (front-engined) and Europa (mid-engined) road cars, but they had also taken over the machine

The first mid-engined Lotus road car was the Renault-powered Europa announced at the end of 1966. It was a smoothly-shaped, but small car, and strictly a two-seater.

The interior of the 1970 Lotus Europa, showing that familiar low roofline and the high central 'services' tunnel between the seats, which, of course, hides the deep backbone frame.

Open-plan office work at Hethel, soon after the new factory had been opened. The Europa is parked on the carpet near the front doors, and the Directors' offices are in the background.

One of the first projects of Lotus' current Managing Director, Mike Kimberley, was the Europa Twin-Cam, which involved mating the twin-cam Lotus-Ford engine to the Europa's structure. To improve rearward visibility for the driver, the 'sail' panels on the rear quarters of the shell were cut down.

16

The most powerful Europa derivative of all, regrettably only a one-off prototype, was GKN 47D, which was powered by nothing less than a 3.5-litre light-alloy Rover V8 engine. There hasn't been a V8-engined Lotus production car . . . yet.

tools and jigs for production of the twin-cam cylinder heads; Villiers, who had recently taken over JAP, continued to assemble the engines for the first year or so.

Before long the total factory floor space had grown to 350,000sq ft (glass-fibre body manufacture had originally been in old airfield outbuildings, but was soon brought into a new facility), and Colin Chapman had taken the opportunity to complete the full range of 1960s models, for in 1967 the Elan Plus 2 was revealed. This was a smooth fixed-head coupe model which effectively used a longer-wheelbase version of the two-seater Elan chassis, but was the first Lotus to offer 2+2 seating accommodation. The new model was more up-market than the Elan, and it signalled the way in which Chapman wanted his company to develop in the next few years. He wanted to move away from the original Lotus image, of producing proprietary-part kit cars in cramped and rather crudely equipped factories — and he wanted to produce increasingly more prestigious machines.

Even so, the Elan Plus 2 was on offer as a kit car as well as a fully assembled machine, though the proportion of fully assembled Plus 2s increased steadily in the next few years. It may be of interest to recall its principal features which, apart from the backbone chassis with all-independent coil-spring suspension, included front and rear disc brakes, rack-and-pinion steering and centre-lock pressed-steel wheels. There was also the well-known Lotus-Ford twin-cam engine, tuned to produce up to 118bhp (net), and those truly elegant looks.

The Plus 2's wheelbase was 8ft 0in, the unladen weight about 2,085lb and the original retail price for a built-up example was £1,923. Independent road tests soon showed that it had a top speed of 118mph and could often reach 30mpg (Imperial) in day-to-day motoring.

For the next few years company expansion was rapid. Until the late 1960s Lotus had been privately owned — almost entirely by Colin Chapman and his immediate family — but from October 1968 it was floated off as a public company. The original Board of Directors comprised Colin Chapman (as Chairman and Managing Director), Fred Bushell (Finance Director and Company Secretary), and Peter Kirwan-Taylor, who was now a power in the land with a merchant bank in the City of London. A few months later Dennis Austin was hired, as Lotus' Managing Director. It is important, even in a marque history like this, to

A display exhibit of the original Lotus-Ford twin-cam engine, with Mundy-designed top end and Ford cylinder block and moving parts. The gearbox featured a Ford casing, but special close-ratio internals and — in this case — a very strange-looking lever.

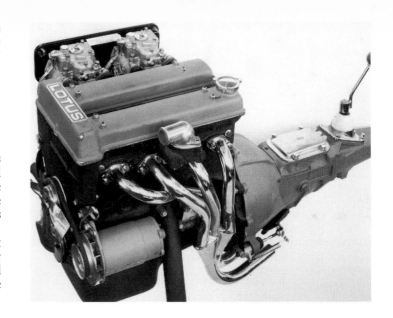

realize that the parent company was Group Lotus Car Companies Limited, and it controlled everything in which the resourceful Chapman had an interest, while Lotus Cars Limited was the wholly-owned subsidiary which was responsible for building the road cars. Then, as ever afterwards, the activities of Team Lotus were entirely separate from those of the road car concern.

I think it is important to the story of the Elite, Eclat and Esprit models to summarize how the company developed before they were born, and I feel that this can most simply be done with the aid of a table, which not only notes annual production, but also the pre-tax profits earned:

Production and profits — 1964 to 1973

Year	1964	1965	1966	1967	1968	1969	1970	1971	1972	1973
Lotus production	1,195	1,234	1,519	1,985**	3,048	4,506***	3,373	2,682	2,996****	2,822*****
Lotus-Cortina production	567	1,118*	986	—	—	—	—	—	—	—
Total production	1,762	2,352	2,505	1,985	3,048	4,506	3,373	2,682	2,996	2,822
Pre-tax profits	£113,000	£154,000	£251,000	£324,000	£731,000	£606,000	£321,700	£736,500	£1,126,700	£1,155,700

* This was the year in which the Lotus-Cortina achieved Group 1 homologation, which required 5,000 cars a year to be built.
** Europa production began early in the year and Elan Plus 2 production began during the summer.
*** The company's all-time record year. Europa sales began in the UK.
**** Plus 1,254 16-valve Type 907 engines delivered to Jensen Motors.
***** Plus 4,008 engines.

However, although profits had risen sharply in the early 1970s, production of Lotus cars had fallen away, and this indicated that something would soon have to be done. There had been no new Lotus 'shape' since the Elan Plus 2 appeared in 1967, and no new chassis engineering, either. There were signs that the enthusiasts were beginning to lose interest in Lotus because they thought that the ideas had run out. Another problem for Lotus was that their twin-cam engine was built on the basis of the 1,499cc Ford cylinder block, which had been superseded in main-stream production by the deep-block (cross-flow) 1,599cc design in 1967.

Something would have to be done? Something *was* being done — and the evidence was all around at Hethel. For the 1970s, Lotus not only had a new engine design in prospect, but new cars as well. It was going to be an exciting, if bumpy, ride.

CHAPTER 2

Lotus for the 1970s

New strategies, new engines, new models

Lotus first considered an eventual replacement for the twin-cam Lotus-Ford engine in 1964 — less than two years after it had first gone on sale — but it was not until 1966 that a clear scheme had evolved. Even then, the intention was that the new unit should be a 2-litre with four valves per cylinder. It was this design which later matured as the 900-Series engine which has powered the modern generation of Lotus road cars.

As Tony Rudd's paper, read to the Institute of Mechanical Engineers in 1973, succinctly summarized it all:

'In the mid-1960s, the company recognized the need for a 150bhp engine to give a low bonnet line, weight and centre of gravity. Such an engine was not commercially available then or in the foreseeable future, so it had to be specially designed, developed and built.'

Steve Sanville was in charge of Lotus' powertrain development in 1966, and he recruited Ron Burr from Coventry Climax for the new project. Since Burr had been involved in the design of the four-valves-per-cylinder Coventry Climax FWMV racing engine and the stillborn flat-16 Grand Prix unit, he clearly knew a lot about the layout of high-performance engines.

The design concept revolved around the slant-4/V8 relationship in which a four-cylinder engine would be installed in the engine bay at an angle of 45 degrees, and a 90-degree V8 could be produced along similar lines with the same bench-mark cylinder bore centres, pistons, connecting rods, cylinder heads and valve gear. The smaller engine was always intended for use in road cars, whereas the V8, while attractive if Lotus had a true Supercar in mind, was more useful as a basis for an Indianapolis 500 (4.2-litre) racing unit.

(Lotus had strong Indianapolis links with Ford of Detroit at the time, but then, Colin Chapman always *did* have visionary ideas of his own. . . .)

At the concept stage, when no money had yet been spent on hardware, the team also considered 2-litre V6 layouts — one with a 60-degree angle (which was too high), the other with 120 degrees (too wide) — from which we may assume that an 'Indy' project would then have been a V12. Once a slant-4/V8 combination had been settled, work began on the cylinder head (this often happens with *ab initio* engine work), with the detail of the block and bottom end to be tackled later. Even in 1967 the chosen design was that which has served Lotus so well for so many years — it was to be an 'over-square' engine, with twin overhead camshafts, four valves per cylinder and a camshaft drive by an internally toothed cogged belt.

It was at this stage that Chapman, Sanville and Burr visited the Earls Court Motor Show in October 1967, inspected the brand new slant-4 Vauxhall road car engine and were amazed to see that its bore centres were exactly the same as those which Lotus were preparing to use. A lightly modified prototype Lotus head could be persuaded to mate with the Vauxhall block with very little difficulty.

Colin Chapman lost no time in negotiating the use of Vauxhall blocks for his designers' use, which must have caused Ford eyebrows to be raised. However, it was always made clear to me that this was only done to 'get the show on the road' — to speed up development of the cylinder head, valve gear and breathing of the design — and that there was never any intention to fix up supplies for future road cars. For years, Chapman had harboured a desire

This small-scale model was pictured in Group Lotus' Company Report for 1972 and captioned 'The Coming Generation?'. Perhaps, at one time, it might have been the planned 2+2 car, but it looks more like a late-1960s Maserati Ghibli than a prototype Eclat.

to build complete Lotus engines, and this resolve stood firm. One day, a 16-valve production engine would be built, but for the moment the cast-iron Vauxhall Victor block would be an ideal 'slave' unit.

At this stage, no doubt, the reader (and the author!) must be in danger of being submerged in type numbers, so I should confirm that while Lotus designers had their own ideas of what the engine should be called, the Marketing Department had another. To the designers, it was the new 900 family, while to Marketing the original engine was the LV220. At the concept stage, the designers' engine family lined up as follows:

Type 904 Iron block 2-litre race engine, with fuel injection
Type 905 Iron block 2-litre road-car engine
Type 906 Sand-cast alloy block 2-litre race engine
Type 907 Die-cast alloy block 2-litre road-car engine
Type 908 Alloy block 4-litre V8 race engine
Type 909 Alloy block 4-litre V8 road-car engine

The Marketing Department, however, announced the Type 904 as the LV220 (LV = Lotus-Vauxhall, 220 = maximum brake horsepower produced), and the Type 906 as the LV240. At the same time, they retrospectively named the Lotus-Ford engines as LF105 and LF115, depending on their power output! Whatever, there was absolutely no way that the new engine could become a production reality before the early 1970s as it would take that long for detail design work to be completed, and for Lotus to instal new machinery to build it. The first 904/LV220 did not run until July 1968, at which point it was fitted with Tecalemit-Jackson fuel injection and had a bore and stroke of 95.25mm × 69.85mm (or, more prosaically, 3.75in × 2.75in in good old Imperial measure), which gave a capacity of 1,995cc. (The bore and stroke of the Vauxhall Victor 2000, by the way, was 95.25mm × 69.24mm and the cubic capacity 1,975cc. Lotus kept the same bore, but used their own special crankshaft, and pushed the swept volume almost to the limit of the 2-litre class.)

New models to replace the existing cars were going to take even longer to develop — especially as Colin Chapman was interested

The definitive Type 907 engine was unveiled in 1971 for fitment to the Jensen-Healey, when it was in 140bhp/1,973cc form. *Autocar's* cutaway drawing, as ever, was the most instructive guide to its construction.

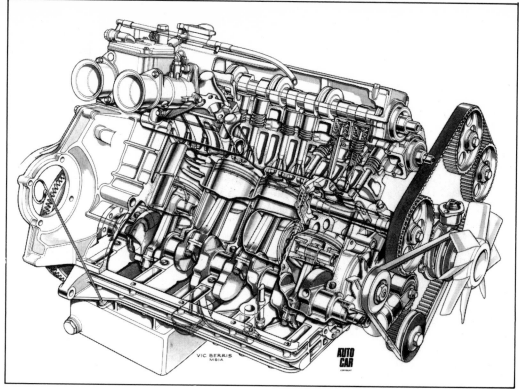

in building not just one, but an entirely new range. Once again, to make sense of the thinking behind the new cars, I must summarize the Lotus range of 1967-68 and their immediate plans for change:

1968 model range

Lotus 7 — Space-frame, starkly trimmed, separate wings and headlamps. Series 3 to be announced in 1968. Produced in kit-form by Lotus Components, and not included in annual totals (see Chapter 1).

Lotus Elan — Series 4 to be announced in 1968, but no major style changes since 1962 and none planned.

Lotus Europa — Series 2 to be announced in 1968 (with bolt-on in place of bonded-in frame) and UK marketing to begin in 1969. No major chassis changes planned.

Lotus Elan Plus 2 — Newly launched in August 1967. No major changes planned, nor convertible version in view.

As far as Colin Chapman was concerned, the Lotus 7 concept had no long-term future. Even though there would be a Series 4 model in 1970, this was to be a last fling, and in 1973 Lotus would hand over all manufacturing rights to Caterham Car Sales.

Replacements, therefore, were to be found for a range

Before the end of the 1960s, stylist John Frayling produced this quarter-scale model as an early M50 proposal. It was smart, but was thought to be too conventional.

comprising front-engined two-seater, front-engined 2+2-seater and mid-engined two-seater. New cars, when designed, would need to be considerably larger, somewhat faster and consequently more expensive than the Elans and Europas. Accordingly, it was highly unlikely that they would sell at the same rate.

(For the record, it is worth noting that when the old models finally dropped out of production in the mid-1970s, no fewer than 12,224 Elans, 5,200 Elan Plus 2s and 9,230 Europas had been built, and the maximum production rate, achieved in 1969, was about 100 cars a week. Things were to change dramatically in the next few years.)

Almost by definition, Chapman's choice of a physically larger, 2-litre engine, rated at about 150bhp, meant that he was abandoning the Elan market. This car, let's never forget, had weighed a mere 1,480lb in its original open sports form and measured 12ft 4in from stem to stern. It had room for only two

occupants. For the 1970s, accordingly, he decreed that two new designs, effectively of the same family and philosophy, were to be laid down. One was to have a front-engined layout and would have a longer wheelbase than the Elan Plus 2 and offer more interior space, while the other would be a pure mid-engined two-seater coupe.

It was going to be a lengthy and costly business, but original plans were upset by a dip in Group Lotus' profitability. At one time, it had been hoped that the first new model could be introduced in 1972, which presupposed that most pre-launch expenditure would have to be made in 1970 and 1971. In 1969, pre-tax profits had been £606,000, but in 1970 they dropped to £321,700 (on total sales of £4,932,000); to keep the ship in balance, capital spending had to be trimmed, and it was not until the 1972 Company Report was published (in mid-1973) that the directors reported that no less than £513,000 had been held back

In the spring of 1971, Oliver Winter-bottom produced an M50-style pro-posal which everyone seemed to like. In April this rather rough-looking model was tested in the MIRA wind-tunnel with very satisfactory results.

The finalized quarter-scale model of the M50, which became the Elite of 1974, was approved in April 1971, and looked almost exactly like the produc-tion car which was to follow.

Three-quarter front view of the quarter-scale model of the M50, showing the close similarity to the final product.

This is the first full-size mock-up of the M50 Elite, in wood and glass-fibre, photographed in September 1971. Lotus' first thoughts were right, in every detail respect.

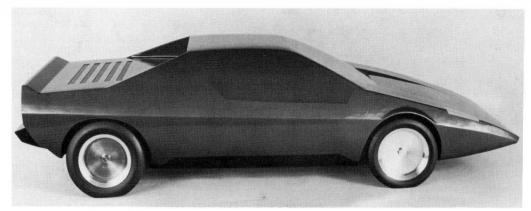

Even while Ital Design were working on the very first Esprit, Lotus' Oliver Winterbottom was working up his own ideas on the subject. It was a very smart wedge indeed, with a very prominent spoiler across the tail. Was it potentially as attractive as the Italian Esprit? Some say it could have been.... This was only a scale model, of course.

and that 'this amount almost wholly relates to the design and tooling of the 2-litre engine and the new generation of cars which we shall be producing for the next five years'.

This was the report which carried three mystery photographs captioned 'The coming Generation?' — one of which was the 1972 Giugiaro Esprit prototype, one a nose-on view of the new Elite (though not identified as such) and a third being a quite meaningless clay model of a front-engined fastback coupe.

In fact the engine, whose head had been designed in 1967-68, well before work on the cars actually started, was revealed in the autumn of 1971 and went into production early in 1972 (initially for exclusive supply to Jensen for the Jensen-Healey), while the first of the new cars, the front-engined Elite, was not unveiled until May 1974. The mid-engined car took even longer; the prototype style, by Giugiaro on a much-modified Europa Twin-Cam chassis, was seen in 1972, but the production Esprit was not shown to the public until October 1975 and first deliveries did not begin until June/July 1976.

One reason for this was that the designers had to spend a good deal of time fighting to overcome existing and proposed legislation. In any case, the new cars were to be so sophisticated that it was never going to be quick or easy to get them on to the market. Throughout the industry, there is a certain inertia, an unalterable pace, involving suppliers, which not even Lotus could upset.

Naturally, a number of important personalities, in addition to the Chairman, were closely involved with the new projects. The first of the new faces, and an expert to guide the new engine into production, was Tony Rudd. Prior to mid-1969, Rudd had been Chief Engineer of the BRM Grand Prix team for some years (and before that he had been involved in design work with Rolls-Royce at Derby), but the reason for his abrupt resignation from BRM was triggered off by the poor performance of the 1969 team cars and by his abrasive relationship with the team's star driver, John Surtees. Things came to a head at the Dutch GP in June, when the BRMs were almost the slowest cars present. Within a week, Rudd had left BRM — and in September 1969 he joined Lotus. Colin Chapman, whose Lotus GP cars had raced against the BRMs for a decade, knew a good engineer when he saw one and attracted Rudd to Hethel as Manager of the Powertrain Engineering Department. The press release confirming his appointment said that this would 'entail responsibility for the continuing development of current engines and of new production engines for the 1970s'.

Even that was only a short-term appointment, for by 1971 Rudd was Technical Director of Lotus Cars, and on the Board of that company.

In the meantime, the engine was progressing well. Following initial test running in 1968 in cast-iron block form, it was chosen to power the Lotus 62 mid-engined racing sports cars, which

John Frayling suggested that this was one way of converting the hatchback Elite M50 into the M52. In this form it could surely only have been a 2+2 at best, or rather a comfortably spacious two-seater. Although this is a full-size style, it was only a mock-up, which was never made to run, and it dates from about 1973.

looked similar to the existing mid-engined Europas, but were completely specialized racing machines. In 1969, two of these cars, driven by John Miles, Brian Miur and Roy Pike, notched up success after success, for their 220bhp (LV220) slant-4 engines endowed them with remarkable performance. The high point of their season came when John Miles' 62 took third place in the Tourist Trophy race behind a couple of Lola T70s, which were fitted with monstrously powerful Chevrolet V8 engines.

Although this racing programme showed up some weaknesses in the Vauxhall cylinder blocks, the Type 905 cast-iron-blocked engine, in 147bhp form, was completely reliable when used in a Vauxhall Viva GT car and a Bedford CF van for road testing. By 1970, development of the light-alloy engine had progressed so well that it was decided to invest in a major machining and assembly facility for the Type 907 engines at Hethel.

In the meantime, the performance of all existing Elan and Europa models was boosted, effectively to close the gap between the 1960s cars and the mid-1970s models which would eventually replace them. The Lotus-Ford twin-cam engine, rated at 105bhp or 115bhp according to its tune, was re-engineered under Tony

Rudd's control into 'Big Valve' form and was placarded at no less than 126bhp. The Elan, thus powered, became the Elan Sprint, the Plus 2S became the Plus 2S 130, and the Europa Twin-Cam became the Europa Special.

Much of the credit for the development of these models goes to Mike Kimberley, now Managing Director of the company. Kimberley and the author of this book both began their working careers at Jaguar in Coventry, and Kimberley went on to become closely involved in the design of the sensational (but, alas, unraced) 5-litre V12 mid-engined XJ13 sports-racing prototype. He arrived at Lotus in August 1969 as 'Engineer in charge of Continuous Engineering', shortly took on the Twin-Cam Europa project, and soon became Product Engineering Manager, under Tony Rudd.

As Mike now recalls: 'There was already an M50 project when I joined the company, but that was scrapped by 1971 and we started on another car.' This confirms what I have also been told by Paul Haussauer, who had worked at Lotus before leaving to start the Clan Crusader project of his own.

Even today, many enthusiasts become confused between the

The first M52 prototype, pictured on November 5, 1974, when it still carried the badging of 'Elite Coupe' and slightly different rear moulding details.

two series of Lotus type numbers and, in truth, so have Lotus themselves in the past: The Lotus 'Mark' (later 'Type') number system began, way back, when Colin Chapman built his first Austin 7 Special, and it progressed through such famous cars as the original Elite (Type 14), the first mid-engined race car (18), the Elan of 1962 (26) and the Lotus-Cortina saloon (28). By the end of the 1960s the Elan Plus 2 was the 50 (confusing!), and the famous wedge-styled 1970 GP car was to be the Type 72. The build-up of such numbers persists to this day.

Lotus road-car 'M' or model family numbers are completely different. M50 refers to the complete family of front-engined 1970s/1980s-style Elite/Eclat/Excel cars (M50, M52 and M55 respectively), whereas M70 refers to the modern mid-engined variety. The fact that each sub-derivative of the cars also gets an old-style Type number (the original 1974 Elite was Type 75, for instance) only adds to the complication, and the fact that the Type 79, according to Lotus, was not only the famous ground-effects Formula 1 car of 1978, but the Esprit S2.2 as well makes some of us throw up our hands in despair. At least Lotus staff and executives seem to know what they are all talking about!

The definitive M50 car came together quickly during 1972, with Tony Rudd in charge of the project, Mike Kimberley overlooking mechanical design and Oliver Winterbottom masterminding the styling. It was mostly an 'evenings and weekends' job for the top men, who had many other things to interest them in normal working hours. The thinking behind the new cars was summed up for me by Mike Kimberley, with whom I viewed the wooden mock-up in 1972:

'Colin conceived all three cars — Elite, Eclat and Esprit — as a package, and decided that we should move up-market to a new sector, based on price, mainly to give ourselves more protection, for other manufacturers were beginning to move into the sector we were already in. If we chose to continue with the old models, which had already been in production for a long time, it would have meant spending £1 million, say, just to homologate the Europa in certain countries. The cost didn't seem logical without doing a new model.'

I asked him if it had not been enormously brave to do a new car, a new engine and a new style, all at the same time?

'It was incredibly brave, and personally I would not try to do it

27

again. When an important requirement is to maintain high quality and reliability we should change the minimum to achieve the perceived improvement which is necessary. But here we were faced with exceptional circumstances, for in every case our existing cars were becoming out of date, especially from a legislation point of view.'

It was in the same discussion, incidentally, that Mike confirmed that the *minimum* production period considered was that the cars should be built for eight years, and that the engine or its developments should last for much longer than that.

At the beginning of the 1970s, Group Lotus was building up sales and profits steadily, to ensure that investment in the new range of cars could be financed internally. Profits jumped back from £321,700 in 1970 to £736,500 in 1971, to £1,126,700 in 1972 and to £1,155,700 a year later. Colin Chapman and his co-directors (in 1973 they were Sir Leonard Crossland, Fred Bushell and Peter Kirwan-Taylor) were confident that they could steer Lotus into a higher and more prestigious market sector, though they also realized that unit sales must fall.

In the meantime, certain major policy changes were being made known. The entry of the United Kingdom into the European Economic Community in 1973 meant that the country had to accept the principle of applying Value Added Tax to goods and services, rather than adding Purchase Tax to a more limited range of goods. This meant that VAT had to be applied to cars *and* car parts alike, so there was no longer much justification in selling cars as kits to avoid taxation (which, under Purchase Tax rules, was possible). However, even before this new set of laws was enacted, Lotus had begun to discourage the sales of kits (or, rather, to encourage the sale of built-up Lotus models), and it was always made clear that there would be no question of kit supply for the next-generation cars.

From the start of Type 907 engine production, Lotus emphasized how 'clean' the unit was in USA-emissions terms, pointing out that the Stromberg carburettor-equipped version would meet 1974 regulations without the need for any extra 'hang-on' equipment, and that even the very stringent rules proposed for 1976 would also be in reach with little more than a 'clean air package' added to the basic engine.

In the course of a revealing interview which he gave to *Autocar's* Ray Hutton in October 1972, Colin Chapman said:

'America has only ever been about a quarter of our market; roughly half of our production is for the home market, a quarter for Europe and a quarter for America . . . The way legislation is going in America from here on I don't think it is necessarily going to produce safer cars. Not only us, but the majority of European car manufacturers, are beginning to feel the same and we are becoming more concerned with meeting the EEC requirements than the American regulations.'

In addition, although he was not to be drawn in detail, he almost spelled out Lotus' future marketing policy:

'As a company with a sporting image, we should always have a model in our range of a more advanced sporting nature such as a mid-engined two-seater, but not to the exclusion of more conventional designs. Our current range — a front-engined two-seater, a front-engined four-seater and a mid-engined two-seater — is the sort of line we will continue with.' (There was something of a white lie here, for the Eclat was more of a generous 2+2 than a two-seater, but other forecasts have all come to pass.)

There was more to come in the same interview when Ray Hutton asked if future Lotus cars would be 'softer' than before? 'Yes. Our objective is to produce a very comfortable high performance car and anything that makes the environment of the car easy and more pleasant, like automatic transmission, power steering, standard air conditioning, etc, will all be incorporated in future Lotuses.'

With a Chairman like that, Lotus really did not have to worry about keeping their future intentions secure, for he was giving away almost every secret except the date of announcement, the price and the styling of the new models! In fact, we all had to wait until 1974 for the first new-type Lotus to appear. It was an exciting and significant time for all those at Hethel. Lotus was changing direction, and the impact on the company and its potential customers was enormous. The fact that the new car went into production almost precisely when the world of motoring was knocked sideways by the first oil shock of 1973-74 didn't help. It all led to a combination of circumstances which nearly sunk Lotus for good.

CHAPTER 3

M50 — the new Elite

Lotus goes hatchback

Lotus planned to announce the first of their new generation of cars, the hatchback front-engined four-seater which had been christened Elite, in March 1974, and had placed advertisements accordingly. Then in February the miners went on strike, the Government imposed a three-day working week to save electricity and the launch of the new car was delayed until mid-May. The problem was that one long-lead advertisement in the *Sunday Times* magazine could not be cancelled, and it appeared in March, to the embarrassment of Lotus and the hilarity of the motoring business!

The advertisement urged people to 'Join the Elite', and most motoring writers seemed to think that it was, indeed, a splendid new car. The reliability problems of the *original* Elite had been forgotten many years earlier, and attention was focussed on the car's engineering and novel features.

Much of it was expected — such as the use of a simple, backbone chassis and the 16-valve Type 907 engine, backed by the Lotus five-speed gearbox (with BL Maxi gears and manufacture by Beans Industries in the West Midlands) — and it would have been quite unthinkable for a new Lotus not to have all-independent suspension, rack-and-pinion steering and a glass-fibre bodyshell. The style, too, was a nicely detailed and conceived wedge, with a well-raked screen and two passenger doors.

The major innovation, which made a real talking point, was that the bodyshell was arranged to have a glass hatchback, rather like that of the Reliant Scimitar GTE, but done in a more shapely manner, and that there was even more passenger accommodation than had been expected. Under that glossy skin, too, there were rear drum brakes (the Elan and Plus 2 models which were

effectively displaced by the new car both had rear discs), while Colin Chapman's promise of offering full air conditioning was upheld on the more expensive version.

It was revealed that design had begun in March 1971, a full-size styling model had been completed in September and the first running prototype had been commissioned in January 1972, with two further cars finished by April 1972. Tony Rudd and Mike Kimberley had made frequent out-and-back dashes to Monte Carlo during weekends, and the first 10 production cars each notched up 50,000 miles in a matter of months in the course of Lotus' own particular 'type approval' test.

On announcement, several other points needed to be emphasized, though Lotus kept relatively quiet about their revolutionary new method of moulding the major GRP body sections for a while. (This used injection moulding of resin to the laid-up mat, and was fully protected by worldwide patents.)

Naturally, there were steel beams in the doors, so that the Elite could meet the latest American side-intrusion regulations, but for the first time on any car these were neatly integrated, linking the hinges at the front of the doors to the locks and catches at the rear and supporting the door frames in the centre. It helped, of course, that the Elite was designed *after* the legislation had been published, so the beams were not afterthoughts of a simpler layout.

The enormous windscreen was cleared by a single wiper blade, pivotted in the centre of the body, and naturally there was also a wiper on the hatchback glass as well. Lotus made the point that the general styling of the car was theirs, and theirs alone, but they did admit that Giugiaro (who was working on the new Esprit,

The basic Lotus backbone chassis-frame, as evolved for the front-engined Elite and Eclat models, was simple to tool, but massively strong. In recent years it has been galvanized before assembly — a process which makes it virtually rust-proof. Since the early 1960s, all Lotus road cars have had this type of chassis.

Chassis assembly, by welding up the simple pressings and foldings, is carried out at the Hethel factory on simple jigs and fixtures.

though few people knew this yet) had been consulted about the interior trim and layout. Even though the car was released before the time when journalists took much notice of drag coefficients, Lotus let everyone know that MIRA's wind-tunnel had produced a C_d figure of a mere 0.30 with the front under-nose spoiler, or 0.33 without a spoiler. It was an astonishingly low figure by almost any standards.

The new Elite gave us our first sight of the definitive Type 907 engine, as the company intended to use it in their new generation of cars. Like those units already being supplied to Jensen, its alloy-block/alloy-head construction featured four valves per

cylinder, opposed at 38 degrees, with a pent-roof combustion chamber and ideally positioned central spark plug. Carburation on the European/UK market cars was by twin horizontal dual-choke Dellorto DHLA 45 instruments, the compression ratio was 9.5:1 and camshaft overlap around Top Dead Centre was 50 degrees, with a maximum lift of 0.360in. By comparison, the US-specification 'Federal' cars had twin sidedraught Zenith-Stromberg 175CD 2SE carburettors, a compression ratio of 8.4:1, camshaft TDC overlap of 52 degrees and a maximum lift of only 0.250in.

In European-specification tune, the engine developed 160bhp

31

The Elite/Eclat front-engined chassis, almost ready for final assembly to begin. Notice the steel backbone wrapped closely round the engine and gearbox.

The front-engined chassis, with its drive line and suspension units already in place. Note the concentric coil spring/damper units at the rear, the simple rear suspension geometry and the inboard drum brakes.

Final assembly under way at Hethel, with this European-specification Elite or Eclat chassis awaiting the arrival of the glass-fibre body from another department. Or perhaps the body immediately behind it is about to be hoisted into position.

An early example of the Type 907 2-litre engine, complete with cast exhaust manifold, ready for fitment to an Elite or Eclat.

The carburettor side of the Type 907 2-litre engine, complete with two Dellorto dual-choke carburettors, which will eventually have an air box fitted. The distributor is horizontally positioned under the carbs, and the oil filter is close to the distributor.

(DIN) at 6,500rpm. It is worth noting that the engines being supplied to Jensen only developed 140bhp at the same rpm; these engines used DHLA 40 carburettors, had an 8.4:1 compression ratio and used different cam profiles with a mere 42 degrees of overlap.

The five-speed transmission of the new car was as previously used in the Elan Plus 2S 130 model and featured a gear cluster lifted from BL's Austin Maxi car. The casing was machined by Beans Industres, who also assembled the transmission before shipping it to Hethel. When pundits saw that this cluster had to deal with the torque of the new Lotus engine, some of them winced, for it had only been designed by BL to look after a maximum torque of about 100lb ft. Lotus' stressing, however, was sound, for the box always stood up well to its task in the Elite.

At the back of the car, the chassis-mounted final drive was a proprietary Salisbury 7HA unit, massively strong, but not always very refined or quiet in its operation. When the new car was launched, the ratio was 3.73:1, but it was not long before a 4.1:1 ratio was standardized in its place, with the higher gear remaining as an option. One reason for this change was that the production engines did not develop quite as much power and torque as had been hoped (and the cars were, perhaps, a little heavier than they might have been) — the classic way to improve acceleration in such circumstances is to lower the overall gearing.

By Lotus standards, the rolling chassis layout could be described as conventional, but it was more advanced than many of the competitors' products. The big box-section backbone frame enclosed the engine and transmission at the front and supported the final drive at the rear. The front suspension was by coil springs and wishbones, with an anti-roll bar, and at first some of the

The Type 907 2-litre engine in de-toxed Federal guise, with two Zenith-Stromberg carburettors instead of dual-choke Dellortos. The car for which this engine is destined has no air-conditioning, or power steering — the belting is much too simple for that!

components were those of the current Triumph Spitfire GT6. (As the years progressed and the cars were developed, however, Lotus took on more of the original design.) Naturally, the steering, by Burman, was a rack-and-pinion unit, and although it was not power-assisted, this feature was promised for future derivatives of the car.

The independent rear suspension layout bore a passing resemblance to that of the mid-engined Europa, but none at all to the Elans in that there was a fixed-length drive shaft, a lower transverse link and a massive pressed-steel semi-trailing radius arm which hinged from the backbone frame under body, ahead of

the rear seats. At the rear, as at the front, there were coil spring/damper units.

The rear drum brakes (with 9 × 2.25in dimensions — the same as the 3-litre Ford Capri) were mounted inboard, on each side of the final drive unit. To maximize the roadholding possibilities, the Elite had die-cast light-alloy wheels (by GKN) with 7in wide rims, and Dunlop Supersport 205/60 VR-14in tyres.

Apart from the Elite's striking good looks, which were helped by the low wedge nose and the hidden headlamps, and its high performance (Lotus claimed a top speed of 128mph, which no independent magazine road-testers could quite achieve), it also

A front view of a European-spec Type 907 engine, with the cogged belt cover/finger guard yet to be fitted. The alternator is on the left in this picture, under the front of the carburettor air box.

had a sumptiously trimmed interior, for which Giorgetto Giugiaro's Ital Design concern had been partly responsible. The profile of the backbone chassis, running down the centre of the car, meant that front and rear seats had to be quite slim and there was no question of more than two people being carried in the rear compartment.

Even so, every trick had been played to make this car into a full four-seater — Lotus' first such car if we discount the Lotus-Cortina, which was really a Ford, after all. One major reason for the choice of a hatchback layout was that the Elite's roof line could be carried further back over the top of the passengers' heads before beginning to dip. Nevertheless, there were limitations inescapable from a compact car with a 97.8in wheelbase and an overall height of less than 4ft. There was 4in less seat-to-roof headroom in the back seats than in the front, though if the front seat passengers were not too tall (and therefore did not need to slide their seats all the way back) there was adequate rear seat space for two adults.

On announcement two versions of the car were put on sale — the Elite 501 being the basic machine and the 502 having extra equipment such as full air conditioning, a more advanced radio/cassette installation and quartz-halogen headlamps. Prices

36

Contrasting engine bay shots of front-engined Elite/Eclat models. For most countries the engine was fitted with twin dual-choke Dellorto carburettors, but where de-toxing was needed (for the USA and Japan, in particular) it was necessary to fit two single-choke Zenith-Strombergs.

A high overhead shot of this 1978-79 Elite shows off the smooth lines and the careful integration of styling details, such as the way the headlamp pod line is linked to that of the air extractor on the bonnet panel. Note that only one windscreen wiper was fitted, and that the front bumper was almost an integral part of the nose of the car.

Among details specially developed for the Elite of 1974 were the distinctive light-alloy road wheels. In this view the windscreen pillars look thick, but visibility from the driving seat was never a problem. There is a small spoiler under the nose.

in the UK were £5,445 for the 501 and £5,857 for the 502 — most customers opting for the more expensive and better equipped derivative.

Incidentally, if these prices look very low by mid-1980s standards (which, in absolute as opposed to index-linked terms, they are), I should point out that the current Jaguar V12 E-Type sold for £3,812, and that the last of the Elan Plus 2S 130/5s was priced at £3,486.

Following its delayed launch, the new Elite went on sale at once, though it could not possibly have been marketed at a worse moment. Even though fuel shortages were easing, all round the world, in the wake of the Yom Kippur war of October 1973 and the massive rise in oil prices which followed it, the demand for cars, particularly fast and notionally thirsty cars, was

Oooh — what big eyes you've got! The headlamps were normally hidden, but flicked upwards, driven by electric motors, when a switch was operated in the cockpit.

The Elite had classic, if somewhat controversial, styling when announced, and was ultimately overtaken in popularity by the more conventionally shaped Eclat. But it was always a car people were proud to have in their garage.

The comprehensive, but simply laid out instrument panel of the Elite/Eclat models — this being a left-hand-drive example destined for the Continent.

Look carefully and you will see that this Elite is fitted with the optional automatic transmission. The bulge in the roof trim above and behind the front seats hides the integral roll-bar.

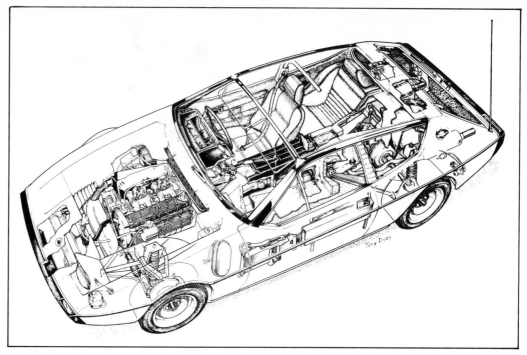

Lotus' own cutaway drawing of the M50 Elite shows, among many other fascinating details, the integrated design of the door beams, the angled installation of the engine, and the semi-estate car hatchback body style.

plummeting.

Mike Kimberley agrees that volumes for the Elite had always been expected to be lower than for the Elan Plus 2 (the company forecast initial production of 25 Elites a week, rising eventually to 35 a week, but that revenue would not be affected as the price-per-car was so much higher. 'Then events rather overtook it. It was a very badly timed oil shock, I agree. Not only that, but we were committed to building the Elite alone until the end of 1975 [*Apart from the last Europas — AAGR*], so we would be a one-model car company, which was a very dangerous position to be in. The oil crisis caused a massive reduction in sales, which made things very difficult for us, but Colin, being far-sighted, continued to invest in new models. That's why we were very fortunate to have the full new range as the energy crisis eased.'

Charts published at the back of this book show that the Elite sold best in its first year (687 cars built), but that the high point of

Elite/Eclat production was 1976, when a total of 797 cars of both types took to the roads. In neither case did this build rate equal the forecast of 25 cars a week, but Lotus forecasters had been unable to foresee how fuel costs and inflation would have rocketed.

Purely for the record, pre-tax profits at Group Lotus plunged from £1,155,700 in 1973 to £293,909 in 1974, and to a loss of £488,000 in 1975, before crawling back to a profit of £17,000 in 1976 and booming up to £556,700 in 1977. These figures show that Mike Kimberley's words are borne out and that Colin Chapman's long-term planning was justified.

Although the 2-litre Elite remained in production for six years, all the important changes and additions to the specification were made in the first 18 months. It was not until the beginning of 1975 that deliveries of the basic 501 model began, by which time the third derivative of the design, the 503, had already been put on sale. The 503 was mechanically similar to the other Elites, but was fitted with the power-assisted steering which had been promised some months earlier.

It was now interesting to try to spot the specification of an Elite by the number of drive belts which could be counted on the front of the engine as it was installed. Apart from the cogged belt to drive the twin overhead camshafts, Elite engines either had one extra vee-belt (the basic model), two belts (power-assisted steering but no air conditioning), or three belts (two different layouts — one for the air conditioning version, the other for cars with the air conditioning plus power-assisted steering). The reason for this, of course, was that power steering required a hydraulic pump on the engine, as did the air conditioning.

The final expansion of the 2-litre range came in October 1975 (at the same time as the Eclat was launched), when the Elite 504 made its bow. This was the most expensive and, as it transpired, the most exclusive Elite, for it was the first-ever Lotus to have an automatic transmission, and all the 503 specification — which included air conditioning and power-assisted steering — was retained. Sales began at the beginning of 1976.

By this time Elite prices were high, and rising, for British inflation was roaring ahead. In the UK, one now had to pay £6,493 for the 501 version, though most customers spent £7,625 for the fully equipped 503. The 504 automatic (the gearbox was a Borg-Warner Model 65, by the way, and the final drive was 3.73:1), complete with its new marcasite trim, cost no less than £7,970.

Although there were small, but unavoidable, losses through the automatic transmission, the Elite 504 was still a fast and impressive car. *Motor* were the only British magazine to test such a car, in 1978 (by which time the retail price had rocketed to £13,020), and they recorded a top speed of nearly 119mph, with 0-60mph and 0-100mph acceleration in 10.4 and 31.6 seconds respectively. Clearly they were impressed, for they called the car 'a comfortable, lavishly finished and equipped, genuine four-seater with superlative road manners, good refinement and, of course, that striking exoticar styling'.

The only possible quibble was that a car of this performance and price really needed something more complex than a four-cylinder engine, but the Elite was so good that this really spoke volumes for the 16-valve Type 907 engine, which was as smooth and silky as any other of its type. By this time, too, the Elite was not only formidably well equipped, but beautifully finished as well, for no other car maker could match Lotus' standards of building GRP coachwork.

The fittings of the 503 (manual) or 504 (automatic) Elites not only included power-assisted steering and air conditioning as standard, but also stereo radio/cassette equipment, an automatic aerial, tinted glass, electric winding windows, front and rear seat head restraints and rear wash/wipe arrangements.

However, the automatic transmission option was not as popular as had been hoped. Original forecasts had been for 25 to 30 per cent extra sales, but instead it added only about 8 per cent. That meant a maximum of 60 or 70 cars a year (Elite *and* Eclat) were being built with automatic transmission, and this was not really enough to justify the extra aggravation of developing, sourcing and servicing the alternative. Although the option has persisted to this day with the Elite, the Excel of 1982 was not offered with automatic transmission.

Even though it was not a particularly light car (*Autocar's* Elite 503 test car of 1975 weighed 2,552lb with a half-full petrol tank, and it had a top speed capability of at least 125mph), the Elite could still be remarkably economical — an advantage which helped it to stay on the scene when the energy crisis and inflation scenario was at its height. *Autocar's* 503 returned 20.9mpg overall, could cruise at a constant 70mph along a motorway (if a policeman was watching!) at 28.6mpg, and the magazine's testers thought that it should have been capable of around 25mpg in give-and-take, day-to-day motoring.

Once the Eclat came on the scene, in 1975-76, demand for the Elite dropped somewhat, for customers now had a choice of similar chassised and performing cars, but production held up remarkably well until 1980 and the arrival of the 2.2-litre engine; a total of 2,398 cars were built in six years, which is still the largest individual total for a model in the modern Lotus series. Well over half of the original 2-litre Elites were delivered in the UK, but more than 350 went to the USA (where the power output of the de-toxed engines was about 140bhp); the details are to be found in Appendix C.

The Elite had a difficult job to do at first, when it was the only 'modern' Lotus road car on sale, but from the autumn of 1975 it was joined by the Eclat. This car was like the Elite, yet different in so many ways, and it helped spread the appeal of the design. It deserves a chapter to itself.

CHAPTER 4

The fastback Eclat

Smoothing the style

Although it was the mid-engined Esprit which stole the show for Lotus in October 1975 (see Chapter 5), the Eclat which was launched at the same time was commercially just as important. Not only did it put a different body style from the Elite on show, while preserving its rolling chassis, but it also filtered into a lower price bracket. Not only were potential Lotus customers offered something different, they were also being tempted with something of a bargain.

Right from the beginning of the 1970s, the Eclat, as it became, was one of the three new models which Colin Chapman had planned — the 'front-engined two-seater' which he had mentioned to Ray Hutton at *Autocar* in 1972. That interview, of course, was given before the Eclat's layout had been finalized, for it was much more than a two-seater. Lotus themselves always called it a 2+2-seater (which acknowledged that it had less interior space than the Elite), although in truth the reduction in rear seat accommodation was minimal, and headroom was actually maintained. The suspicion remains that Lotus dubbed the car a 2+2 to convince prospective customers that the Elite was internally a larger car, and to convince them that the two cars were somehow very different.

In truth, the Eclat was very similar indeed to the Elite, in all but rear styling and layout. When development began it was dubbed the M52 which, according to Lotus tradition, meant that it was evolved from the basic M50, which was the Elite. For a time, and because it was to have a conventional fastback coupe body style, it was to be called an Elite Coupe — there is an illustration in this book of a prototype, suitably badged.

The basic layout and features of the Eclat were exactly the same as those of the Elite, though there were detail differences to be described below. Much of the bodyshell, too, was the same as that of the Elite, except for the rear.

It helps to consider the bodyshell as two large mouldings — upper and lower — sealed together during manufacture around the rather prominent waistband. The lower mouldings of the Elite and the Eclat were identical. The upper moulding shapes, too, were identical from the nose to the top of the B/C post (the pillar behind the doors), and the screen and doors, too, were identical.

On the Elite, however, the line of the roof continued back to a position above and behind the rear seat passengers' heads, where it supported the hinges of the shallow but by no means vertical glass hatchback of this distinctive car. On the Eclat, the roof line began to slope downwards towards the tail above the heads of the passengers (even though, as I have said, the headroom figure, as measured by independent road testers, was not reduced), then blended smoothly into a fastback tail, with a sensibly sized rear window glass and a conventional boot lid. There was no rear spoiler, none being needed for the Eclat to remain stable. Some people, including the author, thought the Eclat looked better than the Elite — certainly no customer was heard to complain about the styling.

Although the shape and the engineering of the Eclat was very similar to that of the Elite, its sales philosophy was very different. In an attempt to bridge the gap between the latest Elites and the Elan Plus 2 which had just been dropped, Lotus were tempted to 'take money out' of the Eclat, and make it cheaper to build and sell. Mike Kimberley cheerfully admits this, and is also delighted to confirm that as a ploy it failed: 'We produced a 520 version of

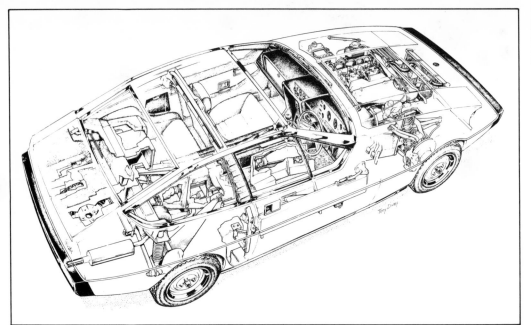

This cutaway drawing shows that the Lotus Eclat was a very generously dimensioned 2+2-seater, or even a full four-seater, if those nominated to ride in the rear were not too bulky.

the Eclat as a basic car. It never caught on, for everybody bought the up-market versions. We now know that most of our prospective customers are individual, entrepreneurial types, who are looking for something different.'

Although the Eclat was launched in October 1975 in 520, 521, 522 and 523 derivatives, only the basic 520 was built at first, with the other versions coming on stream in the spring of 1976. The lowest-specification 520 is interesting, not for its commercial failure (which didn't cost Lotus a bean as there was little original engineering involved), but for what was done to take value out of the package.

An Eclat 520 buyer found that he still had the flashing straight-line performance of other Eclats and Elites, but not the roadholding or the flexibility. Instead of the Lotus/BL five-speed 'overdrive' gearbox, the 520 had a Ford Granada/Capri four-speed box, which was actually bigger, heavier and stronger than the Lotus item, but was also much cheaper. Because it only

had a direct-drive top gear, the final-drive ratio had to be 3.73:1.

Instead of those attractive and distinctive GKN-built alloy wheels, the 520 had pressed-steel wheels with a mere 5.5in rim width, allied to 185/70HR-13in tyres. A look at the parts list confirms that these wheels dated from the mid-1960s and the Lotus-Cortina. Clearly there was less rubber on the road, and therefore the cornering power would be down on that of other Lotus cars, but it was hoped that the lower price tag would make up for this.

The lower price, of course, was important. When it was launched, at the Earls Court Motor Show in October 1975, the Eclat 520 was priced at £5,729, and this compared very well with the £6,483 asked for an Elite 501, and especially with the £7,624 asked for an Elite 503. The 503, of course, had power-assisted steering and full air conditioning, neither of which featured on the Eclat 520, either.

Within months, of course, the Eclat range was effectively

This shot is intended to show off not only the lines of the fastback Eclat, but also the characteristically Victorian styling of Lotus' 'think tank' at Ketteringham Hall. Which do you prefer?

From this view, it is barely possible to identify the fastback Eclat from the hatchback Elite, though one thing is for sure — the car is being cornered *very* hard indeed. This car is one of the earliest examples of the Eclat.

Viewed from the side, the styling of the Eclat was the same as that of the Elite up to the rear of the doors, after which the window and body profiles began to diverge. The Eclat had slightly less rear seat headroom than the Elite, as this picture makes clear, but many customers were not very troubled by this.

complete, for the 524 derivative, with automatic transmission, was also phased in when the other cars went into series production. There is no point in describing the equipment of each version in detail, for they matched the Elites, point for point. There was no downmarket Elite, in fact, but mechanically speaking a 501 Elite was the same as a 521 Eclat, a 502 the same as a 522 and so on. The only significant mechanical variation was that all Eclats were fitted with the 3.73:1 final-drive ratio, whereas the manual-transmission Elites were normally built with a 4.1:1 ratio. The major reason for this was that the Eclat was somewhat lighter than the Elite — perhaps 120lb, if we accurately compare like with like — and it had the same drag coefficient. In addition, there had been a lot of engine development in the previous two years, the 16-valve unit now having different camshaft profiles and significantly higher mid-range torque.

The name Eclat, by the way, is properly pronounced with a silent 't' (phonetically, I suppose, it is spelt 'Ayclaah'), and my *Concise Oxford Dictionary* defines its meaning as 'conspicuous success', or 'social distinction'. It certainly made that sort of impression on the motoring world.

The complications of Lotus type numbers made manifest in the Elite were also obvious in the Eclat. Not only was it M52 on one project list, but Lotus 76 on another. Confused? So you should be, for the Lotus 76 was also the 1974 Formula 1 car . . .

Only 20 Eclats were built in 1975, for series production did not begin until November/December 1975; 16 of these were destined for delivery in Great Britain. Production built up rapidly in 1976 as the full range of derivatives became available and deliveries to North America began. One interesting quirk — which probably proves that we British are pronunciation snobs — is that the USA-market Eclat was not called by its original name, but was simply named Lotus Sprint.

46

The sleek and modern styling of the Eclat has persisted into the 1980s, though the Excel has modified it somewhat. There was a conventional boot and lid, and fastback styling.

Somehow, the Eclat always looks right, from any angle, and in most surroundings. . . .

One of the most characteristic styling features of the Elite and Eclat models was the dip in the window belt line behind the windscreen. Those light-alloy wheels needed attention to keep them clean, but they looked good on the car.

Perhaps there was not a great deal of rear leg-room in the Eclat, but the standard of furnishing was high. Those seats look sumptuously comfortable, and they positively invite you to jump in and command the driver to make for the Mediterranean.

Lotus press material claims that it was a result of the first year's marketing experience in the USA that the Eclat Sprint of 1977 (which is not directly to be confused with the USA-variety of Lotus Sprint) came on to the scene. This survey, Lotus said, 'indicated a demand for a more aggressive option model to be added to the Eclat family'.

Strictly speaking, the Sprint wasn't, for there were no engine changes to it to make it faster than before — which is to say that the finalized 160bhp, 1,973cc engine, complete with E-camshaft profiles and a 60-degree TDC overlap, was retained. Mechanically, the only change likely to make the car 'sprint' faster than the original was that the final-drive ratio on five-speed transmission cars was lowered (raised numerically) from 3.73:1 to 4.1:1.

Only the 520 and 521 derivatives were produced in Sprint form, the 520 Sprint keeping its four-speed Ford gearbox and 3.73:1 final-drive ratio, but having a new design of 5.5in wide cast-alloy road wheels, and the 521 Sprint having the 4.1:1 ratio, the usual type of 7in rim Lotus road wheels, and a mph/1,000rpm figure down from 22.9 to 20.8 in fifth.

All Sprints were white, and in profile were distinguished by

The Eclat Sprint of 1977 wasn't really, for the engine tune was unchanged, at 160bhp. However, the axle ratio was lowered (raised numerically) and there was a modicum of special equipment.

black decorative flashes along the sides, just below the waistline, with the 'Sprint' decal behind the front wheelarch cutouts. There was also a broad black bonnet flash, the boot and fuel filler caps were also blackened, and there was a distinctive Union Flag/Sprint decal on the rear panel of the car. Interiors were either in black, or oatmeal and black.

The Eclat Sprint was an additional model — in current jargon, a 'special limited edition' — and the unadorned Eclats continued unchanged. It was interesting to see how the Sprints were priced, *vis-a-vis* the normal Eclats, when they were announced in February 1977. Prices quoted are *total* UK:

Eclat 520 £7,544   Eclat Sprint 520 £7,842
Eclat 521 £8,074   Eclat Sprint 521 £8,372

— the price premium in each case was £298.

It is interesting to see that with the Eclat, as with the mid-engined Esprit (described in more detail in the next chapter), Lotus production was booming ahead. Only 479 cars had been built in 1975 (all but 20 of which were Elites), but this figure rose to 935 in 1976 and surged forward to 1,070 in 1977, with further expansion to come. It was no wonder that Lotus were happy with their figures, and that they revealed the building of the 50,000th Lotus engine (the majority of which had been Ford-based twin-cams) in May 1977.

There was no doubt that the customers and the battle-hardened magazine testers all liked the Eclats, *Motor* going so far as to headline its 1976 test 'The best Lotus yet'. *Autocar*, that paragon of exactitude, tested an Eclat 523 in July 1977 and found that its maximum speed was 129mph, and that it could achieve 126mph in fourth gear, when the engine was revving past its peak at 6,900rpm.

49

This side view of the Eclat Sprint 520 shows the extra decoration along the flanks, which included the use of a black fuel filler, and the new design of 5.5in rim cast-alloy wheels to replace the basic car's pressed-steel wheels.

What was even more interesting was that the testers of *Car*, Britain's most outspoken monthly motoring magazine, double-tested the same (*Autocar*) Eclat against a Porsche 924, and were in no doubt about their impressions: 'It's a straight no-contest between the 1978 924 and the 1978 Eclat. The Lotus outperforms it, outcorners it, is roomier, more comfortable, quieter at high speed, and very much smoother all the time . . . The Lotus has a refined, elegant, nature; it is fast but it is silky and subtle too, the sort of car you caress rather than just drive. That puts it on a plane beyond the normal 2.0-litre level.'

The only problem, in fact, was that the Lotus was beginning to look very expensive, for at the time the Porsche 924 sold for £7,350 whereas the Eclat 523 was listed at no less than £10,852. In the next few years, the three bogeys of price, depreciation and doubts over Lotus quality control were going to hit the company very hard.

My colleague Ray Hutton, Editor of *Autocar*, actually ran an Eclat 521 for 24,000 miles between 1978 and 1981, a long relationship that was not by any means totally relaxed. In the first 12,000 miles, the car impressed almost everyone with its sparkling performance and fine handling, but depressed its owners by shedding its throttle linkage, having the headlamp actuation fail, and suffering an inoperative cooling fan. Even so,

the Eclat was lovable enough for Ray to dub it an 'All-year-round car'.

The second 12,000-mile stint was not as enjoyable, partly because the car was involved in an accident which, even though it only involved damage to the bodyshell, and none at all to the chassis, was extremely expensive to repair. There was also the fact that the clutch needed replacement at 20,000 miles, that the engine cooling fan electric motor failed again, the alternator broke down and the bodyshell leaked water. *Autocar's* Eclat, in fact, confirmed what a lot of people were saying about the modern Lotus — that although the specification looked as exciting as the styling of the cars, it was not always backed up by reliability in service. What had been excusable when a Lotus was a 1.6-litre machine and kit-built was no longer acceptable when the cars were totally built by the factory and priced well above the levels of the equivalent Porsche.

Even so, the Eclat consistently outsold the Elite in export markets, though not at first in the UK, even though it was not the most charismatic, headline-stealing model in the current Lotus range. Without any doubt, that honour went to the Esprit. Then, as now, the Esprit was the car which any red-blooded Lotus-lover wanted to own.

CHAPTER 5

Lotus + Giugiaro = Esprit

Mid-engined flair

In 1970, Tony Rudd had recommended the design of two major new Lotus models. The first, the M50, was the front-engined Elite already described, and the second was the M70, a mid-engined machine intended to take over the mantle of the Europa. M70 was always envisaged as a two-seater fixed-head coupe, with something of a wedge theme in its shape, and it was always intended to use as much as possible of the new running gear being developed for the M50/M52 Elite/Eclat cars. Like the M50 and M52, the new mid-engined M70 was given approval by management, though there was no way that design work on the new car could begin at once. Lotus' resources were still quite slender, and management first chose to concentrate on finalizing the Type 907 engine and the development of the front-engined cars.

The launch of a new design of mid-engined Lotus looked so remote that there was time for the Europa to be redesigned, not once but twice. Mike Kimberley was given the job of transforming the Europa, which he duly did, and in the autumn of 1971 the Renault-engined S2 was dropped in favour of the Europa Twin-Cam, a similar-chassised car powered by the 105bhp version of the Lotus-Ford twin-cam engine. This new car also featured a restyled rear bodyshell which offered better rear and three-quarter rear visibility, and it had cast-alloy road wheels, though the existing Renault four-speed gearbox was retained.

The new Twin-Cam (which was Type 74 in the Lotus scheme of things) had a top speed of 117mph, 0-60mph acceleration in 7.0 seconds and typical fuel consumption was about 25mpg (Imperial), a considerable improvement on the Renault-engined car. However, the Twin-Cam had a short life, for just one year later, in the autumn of 1972, it gave way to the Europa Special, which was effectively an uprated version of it, with the more powerful, 126bhp, 'Big-Valve' engine and a five-speed Renault gearbox. Performance was boosted yet again, this time to provide the little car with a top speed of 125mph, and 0-60mph acceleration in 6.5 seconds. It set a very high standard indeed, and whatever was chosen to replace it would have a very difficult job to do.

In two distinct ways, however, it was going to be fairly easy to improve on the Europa — in the styling of a new car, and in the space offered to the passengers. The Europa, while always being immediately recognizable, had never been considered as an outstandingly attractive car, and even in its final developed guise it was most certainly not equipped with a very spacious cockpit. Like the two-seater Elan which preceded it, the Europa was a motoring machine rather than a passenger car. The M70, when it came along, would have to be more practical than this.

The styling of the new car, if not its engineering, got under way in 1971, following a chance meeting between Giorgetto Giugiaro, of Ital Design, and Colin Chapman at a motor show. Even in the early 1970s, Giugiaro had a formidable reputation as a stylist/designer, having started his career at Fiat, before moving on to Bertone, then Ghia, prior to setting up his own business, Ital Design, in 1968. Chapman knew all about Ital Design, and *everyone* knew about Lotus, so there was never any lack of understanding between the two. Quite simply, it seems, Giugiaro wanted to know if he could work up a special body style on a Lotus, and Chapman, with the M70 in mind, agreed to let him work on the basis of the mid-engined Europa.

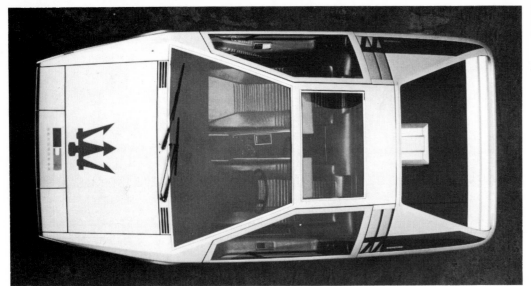

Perhaps this car was one of the inspirations for the shaping of the Esprit by Giugiaro — the Maserati Boomerang of 1972, based on the running gear of the mid-engined Maserati chassis. It was first seen at Geneva in March 1972.

The first Lotus-chassised Esprit, actually being on a much-modified Europa Twin-Cam chassis, which Giorgetto Giugiaro showed on his Ital Design stand at Turin in November 1972. The screen on this first car was even more sharply raked than the production cars were ever to be. The Maserati Boomerang alongside the Esprit shows signs of the same style thinking by the talented Italians.

Giugiaro had already produced the attractive mid-engined Bora for Maserati, and was working on the very angular, but startlingly advanced Boomerang project on the same chassis, so he was familiar with the challenges inherent in mid-engined layouts. To put it baldly, the very first Giugiaro style for Lotus was on the basis of a much-modified Europa Twin-Cam chassis, but since the Type 907 engine was soon to be installed, and the track and wheelbase dimensions were also altered, it is easy to see how Colin Chapman's mind was working. The Europa's wheelbase was 7ft 7in, and its widest track was 4ft 5.5in. Equivalent dimensions planned for the M70 (which did not have a name at this stage) were 8ft and 4ft 11.5in, respectively, so it was not surprising that the chassis supplied to Italy, thus lengthened and widened, was not Lotus' final word on the subject.

Work began on the style in mid-1971, and was completed before the end of that year, not as a running car, but as a full-size mock-up in display trim. A second car, not only with doors which opened, but with a more advanced and integrated design of chassis, followed in 1972. It was the original silver-painted car (now remembered at Lotus, logically enough, as 'the Silver car'!)

The interior, driving position and instrument layout (mainly mock-up) of the original Europa-based Esprit of 1972 with, would you believe, pedals which pivot on the floor? Nevertheless, an amazing amount of this concept was carried over to the production car of 1976.

Another view of the original silver Europa-based Esprit of 1972. There were, of course, many differences in detail style between this car and the definitive version. Apart from the rake of the screen, note the type of louvre behind the nose panel, the twin wipers and the way in which the rear of the body was arranged to open.

With neither help nor hindrance from Lotus, the British stylist Bill Towns (famous, among other things, for his work with Aston Martin-Lagonda) produced this comprehensive restyle of the Europa Special in 1975 and retained the centre section, screen and doors. It was smart, but unsensational, and was not adopted for production.

which made its public debut on the Ital Design stand at the Turin Motor Show of November 1972. Even at this stage, Giugiaro had dubbed it the 'Esprit' (*Concise Oxford Dictionary* definition: Sprightliness; wit), and students of styling evolution will want to be reminded that it stood alongside the Maserati Boomerang project at that show.

At this time, it was interesting to see Colin Chapman explaining it away to the press as 'an exercise on the basis of the Lotus Europa, to combine good styling with practical safety requirements . . .', when at almost the same time he was giving an interview to *Autocar's* Ray Hutton in which he commented that: 'We should always have a model of an advanced sporting nature, such as a mid-engined two-seater.'

Something, for sure, was already on the move, and it wasn't long before motoring enthusiasts began to put two and two together. Mike Kimberley recalls that Lotus' reaction to the completed prototype Esprit was so favourable that a design and development team was immediately set up to work with Giugiaro and they stayed in Italy for at least 18 months. Chapman and Kimberley flew to Turin at least twice a week, during which the body style was refined and turned into a producable proposition.

After the tremendously favourable public showing of 1972 there was a considerable lull while mechanical design got under way, though in the Group Lotus company report published in mid-1973 one of the three pictures published under the heading 'The Coming Generation?' was of the Giugiaro prototype, which had already been adopted by the company. The first true production protytype was nearly completed by Christmas 1974, and was actually driven to London's Heathrow Airport to meet Colin Chapman when he returned from the Argentine Grand Prix in January 1975. By this time, indeed, Lotus had confirmed that the Esprit would be launched during 1975.

To provide more interior passenger space and to allow for the use of the more bulky Type 907 engine, the wheelbase of the M70 was to be 8ft, or 5in longer than that of the Europa which it would replace. It was also destined to be a much wider car than the Europa, though it was always intended to feature a steel backbone chassis-frame. As with the front-engined cars, the engine would be rated at 160bhp (DIN) and would be installed with the cylinder block leaning over at 45 degrees to the left side of the chassis.

Right from the start, Lotus' biggest problem was to find a suitable gearbox, and this was critical to the entire project. Since

What is a car like this doing in a Lotus book? The answer is that the Citroen SM Coupe, complete with front engine and front-wheel drive, used the same basic transmission which has been fitted to every Esprit built since 1975. In the case of the SM, however, the gearbox was ahead of the line of the front wheels.

The definitive original-production Esprit, of 1975, as revealed in this Lotus-prepared cutaway drawing, shows how the engine was placed ahead of the line of the rear wheels, but behind the passenger cabin, and the gearbox was behind the rear wheels and under the rather small luggage compartment. The car was arranged strictly as a two-seater, and there has never been a convertible Esprit production car — all those built having this wedge-styled coupe shell.

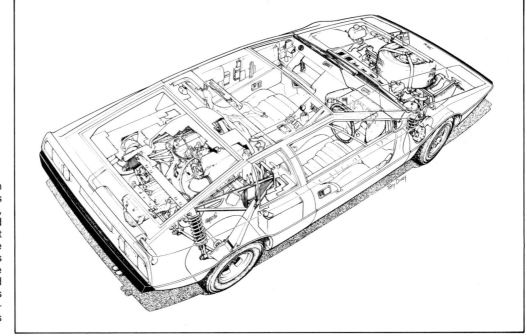

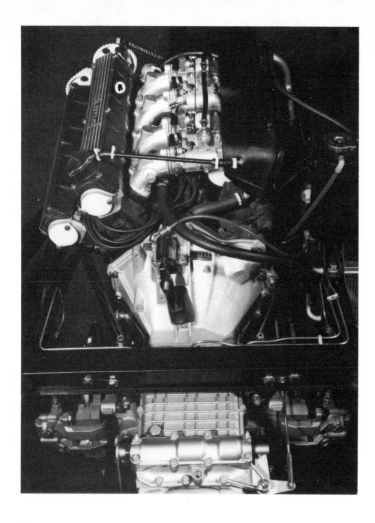

Brand new and sparkling — the engine/transmission installation of the Series 1 Esprit, showing how the gearbox and inboard disc brakes fit under the rear crossmember of the frame.

the Type 907 engine pushed out 140lb/ft of torque, even in 2-litre form (and the highest figure reached by the 'Big-Valve' Lotus-Ford Twin-Cams had been 113lb/ft), it was clear that the five-speed transmission from Renault, as used in the Europa Special, would not be strong enough for the job.

Chapman already knew that it was not financially viable for Lotus to design, tool and build their own transaxles (the five-speed gearbox for the Elite/Eclat cars used standard British Leyland gear clusters) for the cost of tooling up for cutting gears was immense, so Lotus had to look around for an off-the-shelf transaxle. At the same time, they had to consider the V8 engine project, which would produce a great deal more torque than the 2-litre 'four'.

Because Lotus were financially independent of any other motoring manufacturer, they could go shopping for a transaxle almost anywhere. But it was not as simple as that. They were looking for a five-speed transmission with not only ample reserves of strength, but one which satisfied their desire for mechanical 'elegance', was light enough, and was guaranteed for continuity of supply for many years to come. In regard to the latter they were very wise, for the search for the transmission began in 1971, the first production units were not fitted until 1975-76, and they are still being used in the mid-1980s.

The search eventually ended when Citroen offered Lotus the use of their five-speed all-synchromesh gearbox/final-drive unit, which was being used not only in the exotic front-engine/front-drive SM coupe model, but also in the mid-engine/rear-drive Maserati Merak coupe.

The timing of the deal was important, for even in 1972 the SM was a young design, at the peak of its popularity, and the Maserati Merak had still not been announced. The SM transmission was a derivative of the five-speed gearboxes available on other large DS saloons and estates, and Citroen were able to offer supplies for at least the next 10 years. Even though the SM is now long dead and the Merak was dropped in the early 1980s, Lotus still have no supply problems from France.

The gearbox was a conventional two-shaft design — conventional, that is, by transaxle standards — with the output to the spiral-bevel final drive from the second shaft. Its crownwheel and pinion design and the final drive casing were such that it could be run the 'right way' or 'wrong way' round (the Citroen SM and

One of the original Lotus press pictures of the Esprit of October 1975, before it was ready to go into production. This shot emphasizes the attractive wedge style, and it also shows off the separate front spoiler (which would not be blended into the styling before the S2 was launched).

Four big and powerful headlamps normally rest, hidden, behind flaps on the bonnet surface, but can be flicked up rapidly to a position where they ruin the aerodynamics!

The interior of the Esprit S1, which in concept is remarkably similar to that of the Giugiaro prototype of 1972.

Twin struts support the Esprit's rear hatch, which provides access to the luggage space and the engine, the latter normally being concealed beneath this moulded plastic cover.

Merak installations, of course, work in opposing directions). A variety of internal ratios and final drive ratios could also be provided. In the end, those chosen for the mid-engined Lotus were the same as to be found in the SM Coupe, the original Merak and the later Merak 2000, but slightly different from those used in the more powerful Merak SS.

With the general layout of backbone frame chosen, the engine and transmission design finalized, and the front suspension basically being the same as that fitted to the Opel Ascona/Vauxhall Cavalier, the rest of the mechanical design soon slotted into place. The independent rear suspension was as simple as possible; the fixed-length drive-shafts doubled as upper transverse suspension links, combined coil spring/damper units were chosen, and large box-section semi-trailing radius arms helped to locate the wheels, along with lower transverse links. Steering was by rack and pinion (but without power assistance — no Esprit, not even the Turbo, has ever needed this), and the dual-circuit Girling brakes had front and rear discs, solid but not

The Esprit S1 looked attractive from any angle. Roughly speaking, this would be the aspect of the car seen by truck and bus drivers — but not for very long!

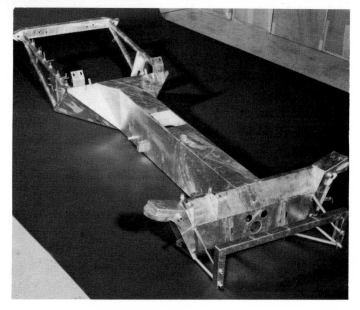

The original design of Esprit chassis-frame (seen here in galvanized form) followed the famous Lotus backbone principle, though the lines did not seem to 'flow' as well as usual towards the rear, which is furthest away from the camera.

ventilated, with the rear discs mounted inboard. There was no servo assistance. Wheels were cast-alloy 14in diameter Wolfrace items, with 7in rims at the rear and 6in at the front.

Much work went into productionizing the startling Giugiaro shape, not only to make it easier and cheaper to build in quantity, but to make it meet all the regulations likely to face such a car in the mid-1970s. The most significant change was to the angle of the windscreen. On the original 'Silver' prototype the screen had been angled back at a mere 19 degrees from horizontal, and to meet the regulations this had to be lifted to 24 degrees 5 minutes. Colin Chapman, however, did not give in without a fight, and the production Esprit still kept the same dramatically swept screen pillars, a feature achieved by making the screen profile much less curved in plan than had originally been intended.

The interior layout and facia style were retained as much as possible and there was a great deal more space for two passengers, but no briefcases or other luggage could be stored in the wide cockpit. There was no space behind the seats, the cover over the backbone chassis-frame, between the seats, was high and wide, and there was only one storage container, ahead of the passenger's knees. As in the Europa, the seats were steeply

Esprit chassis assembly at Hethel, with front suspension build-up partly complete and the engine/transmission assembly already in place. Offering a comparison, a front-engined Elite/Eclat chassis is behind that of the Esprit.

Engine assembly at Hethel towards the end of the 1970s, when production was at its height. Some are for front-engined cars, some for Esprit use. The engine in the mid-foreground already has the Citroen/Maserati transaxle fitted.

Esprit assembly at Hethel, with the rolling chassis already mated with the bodyshells, and with trimming and plumbing well under way. These are all S1 cars, with the separate front spoiler.

reclined, and to climb in and out of the car was not for the modest or the unathletic.

In the meantime, there had been momentous changes at Lotus, both to the fortunes of the company and to the personalities at the top. Dennis Austin, Managing Director of Lotus Cars since 1969, moved on in 1974 and was replaced by Richard Morley, while Mike Kimberley, who had become Vehicle Engineering Manager in 1972, took over the title of Chief Engineer (from Tony Rudd) in 1974 and would be elevated to the Lotus Cars Board at the end of 1975. Tony Rudd became Group Research Director, a position he held until the early 1980s, when he was attracted back into Team Lotus and Grand Prix racing.

The Esprit was not ready for production when it was announced in October 1975, but for several good political reasons Lotus thought it necessary to reveal the car at the same time as the Eclat, which *was* ready. The car, after all, had already been around for three years by then and was known to the public; Lotus

were worried that their customers would despair of it ever being announced if they did not show it then.

As explained in a previous chapter, the combination of energy crisis/oil shock, the launch of the M50 Elite and the progressive withdrawal of the Elan, Plus 2 and Europa families hit Lotus finances very hard. Pre-tax profits in 1973 had been £1,155,700, but they plunged to £293,909 in 1974 and losses were forecast for 1975. Faced with this sort of situation, the company *had* to retrench, and Lotus now confirm that the Esprit was delayed by about nine months due to this financial stringency. In normal circumstances, therefore, the Esprit would have been ready for deliveries to start on announcement in the autumn of 1975. The delay ensured that tooling was not complete by then, the first series production car was not commissioned until May 1976, and deliveries began in June and July.

It is worth recalling that the Esprit's UK price was fixed at £5,844 in October 1975 (when the comparable Elite 501 price was £6,493), but this had rocketed to £7,883, an increase of 35 per cent, by the time deliveries began in the summer of 1976. If Lotus had ever held hopes of producing a direct, but more up-market, replacement for the Europa Special, which had been dropped in 1975, they were now dashed. I doubt if the original published prices of October 1975 were realistic, for company cost accountants do not have to make such huge adjustments in a matter of months.

Few people would now argue with my opinion that the original Esprits were disappointing cars, for they were neither as fast, nor as refined or reliable as Lotus had hoped. For this, Lotus could certainly not blame their suppliers, for the Lotus-built content of the car was approaching 70 per cent by value. The practical limits had already been reached, for the majority of the other 30 per cent went to pay for components such as the Citroen gearbox, wheels and tyres, electrical equipment, springs and dampers.

Lotus claimed that the original Esprit should have reached 138mph, but *Autocar's* test car reached only 124mph, and *Motor* confined themselves to a figure of 'more than 125mph'. This shortfall, however, was not as serious as the lack of refinement in

The 16-valve Type 907 Lotus engine tucked away in the engine compartment of the Esprit S1, before the top cover was fixed in place.

Perhaps this special Esprit wasn't quite as amphibious or versatile as the James Bond film *The Spy Who Loved Me* suggested, but it certainly made very good publicity for Lotus in 1976.

the car, for much of the engine noise was transmitted to the cockpit, and the overall impression was one of harshness. The press, in general, thought that more than three years of development should have seen this ironed out before cars were delivered to customers.

Even so, no-one could argue with the car's remarkably sexy good looks, its handling and general road behaviour, and its general effect on every other motorist — not least the gentlemen in blue! The use of early Esprits in films like the James Bond epic, *The Spy Who Loved Me*, where the car, or things mocked up to look like the car, were made to perform incredible feats, must all have helped.

More than anything else, the Esprit was intended for sale in the United States. Peter Pulver, who was Lotus' principal Stateside distributor, ordered 150 cars at Earls Court in 1976, the first Federal Esprit was commissioned before the end of that year and deliveries began early in 1977. The Type 907 engine, complete with twin Zenith-Stromberg carburettors, came through the emission-reduction tests with such flying colours that the nett power output was still as high as 140bhp, so that the car had a top speed of 120mph in fourth or fifth gears (*Road & Track*, July 1977), all for an East Coast FOB price of $15,990 or — more importantly — $16,844 in California.

The USA launch had a dramatic effect on Esprit production, which had been 138 in 1976, but rocketed to 580 (the best Esprit year ever) in 1977. In 1976 all but four cars were built for the UK, but in 1977 no fewer than 474 were built for the USA.

Nevertheless, criticism and adverse press comment about the original Esprit had struck home, and Lotus made speedy attempts to improve the car. The result was that the S2 model was launched in August 1978, just over two years after the first Esprit deliveries had been made. Second thoughts, in this case, were wise ones, for the S2 was an altogether more integrated package.

Mechanically, there were few changes to the S2 compared with the S1, except that the 'E-Camshaft' specification introduced on late-model S1s was now standardized (with a worthwhile improvement in mid-range torque) and Speedline road wheels replaced the original Wolfrace variety.

Externally, the most obvious improvement to the style was that the front under-nose spoiler was now smoothly integrated into the shape of the car, while slightly protruding engine compartment air intakes were neatly positioned behind the rear quarter windows and at the rear of the car Rover SD1-type tail-lamp clusters were fitted.

Inside and underneath there was a twin electric motor lift mechanism for the headlamps, a new instrument cluster and slide-type switches, recontoured and wider seats, a digital clock, a redesigned engine cover and a revised aluminum-sprayed exhaust system. In case potential customers still couldn't tell the difference, there was an 'Esprit' decal on the nose instead of the 'Lotus' of the first cars and 'Esprit S2' decals on the rear quarters. The UK price, however, had rocketed once again, for our inflation rate was still quite shameful. In August 1978, therefore, the Esprit S2 was priced at £11,124, 9 per cent higher than the last of the S1s. Lotus publicity chiefs were delighted to announce that Team Lotus' contracted drivers, Mario Andretti and Ronnie Peterson, had taken delivery of the first two production S2s.

There was one interesting mechanical innovation, made as much to keep down costs and to minimize the use of front under-bonnet space as for good engineering reasons — the spare wheel now had a 5.5in wide rim and carried a small 185/70HR-13in tyre. It was a mere 'get you home' spare, not intended for prolonged use after a puncture.

Lotus, however, were not content with launching this new derivative, for they also produced a special 'Limited Edition' Esprit S2 at the first NEC Motor Show in October, which was decked out in black and gold 'JPS' livery to commemorate the Lotus 79/Mario Andretti feat of winning both Formula 1 World Championships; 100 of these cars were built, each individually numbered by a plaque on the dashboard, signed by Colin Chapman himself.

S2 performance was nearer to the original claims — *Autocar's* car was good for about 130mph, with 0-60mph acceleration in 8.0 seconds — and the drag coefficient of 0.34 was virtually unaffected by the changes to the style.

All in all, this was a step in the right direction, even if there were still advances to be made in refinement, reliability and overall creature comforts. Lotus had all these things in mind, and the launch of the Chrysler Sunbeam-Lotus in March 1979 hinted at the way they might move next. The Sunbeam-Lotus, after all, had an enlarged 2.2-litre engine. Would in-house Lotus models soon follow this development?

CHAPTER 6

Developing the breed

2.2-litre engines, S2.2 and S3 models

There were major changes at Lotus in the mid-1970s, both organizational and financial, and they all had an effect on the new cars which followed. The group's massive losses of 1975 were stemmed, there was a small pre-tax profit in 1976, and a surplus of nearly £557,000 in 1977. Along the way, the company acquired a run-down Victorian mansion called Ketteringham Hall, which was just a few miles north of Hethel, where Team Lotus, project teams looking after top secret designs, and top management personalities were all installed. Colin Chapman's Deputy Chairman, Sir Leonard Crossland, retired at the end of 1976, and this helped to influence a reshuffle. Colin Chapman himself drew away from day-to-day management of Lotus Cars and began to concentrate on long-term planning. Mike Kimberley, the high-flying ex-Jaguar engineer, became Operations Director in 1976, was virtually running 'Cars' by the end of that year, and was formally appointed as its Managing Director in the summer of 1977.

Shortly after this, the Group became linked with American Express (who had major international banking connections); they not only became principal bankers, but also took an option to buy up to 10 per cent of the share capital. In 1978, Lotus took on the very lucrative, high-pressure, De Lorean design and development contract (see Chapter 10) and they also became involved in the successful, whirlwind, development of the Chrysler Sunbeam-Lotus, which is further described in Chapter 9. This helps to explain why the introduction of redesigned Lotus road cars was delayed until 1980, which in the case of the Elite was six years after the original machine had been launched.

The most important modification in all these revised models was their enlarged engine — from 2 litres to 2.2 litres. When Chrysler approached Lotus early in 1978, no thought had yet been given to enlarging the Type 907 engine, and virtually no built-in 'stretch' had ever been provided by the designers when the unit was conceived in the late 1960s. Because the enlargement for Chrysler (who became Talbot in the summer of 1979) was done so very quickly, it is not surprising that the definitive 2.2-litre for Lotus' own cars was different, in many details, from the engines supplied to Chrysler.

To make the engine larger, it was not practical to increase the cylinder bores, as there was already very little space between adjacent wet liners. The only way, therefore, was to lengthen the stroke, which both Chrysler and (eventually) Lotus were happy to accept, for a longer stroke usually means that an engine develops better mid-range torque, a quality which Chrysler (for their rally car) and Lotus (for more flexible road cars) both found attractive.

To make a 2.2-litre, therefore, the stroke was lengthened from 69.2mm to 76.2mm without the cylinder block having to be changed, and the capacity therefore rose from 1,973cc to 2,174cc. It was no more than coincidental that Vauxhall, with their own slant-4 engine, had also lengthened the stroke to 76.2mm in the early 1970s, for by that time the two units had nothing in common.

The engine used in the Sunbeam-Lotus, its rating and its application, are described in more detail in Chapter 9. At this point, therefore, I need only say that the Sunbeam-Lotus engine, introduced in 1979, was given the Type number 911, while the special-to-Lotus unit was the Type 912. Lotus make the point that the principal differences between the two engines include

There were no major changes to the Elite until the Series 2.2 cars were launched in 1980, and even then there were no major alterations to the style. From this view, the different bumper, the revised and more integrated front spoiler and the slightly changed under-door panels are obvious, together with the wing-flank badges.

The rear aspect of the S2.2 Elite was distinguished by the different bumpers, which housed ribbed tail-lights borrowed from BL's Rover 3500 saloon. There are twin fuel-filler caps — one in each quarter.

A specially liveried Elite S2.2, reminding us that the Grand Prix team use Tissot timing for their cars.

different carburation, cylinder head, camshaft profile, ignition, valve gear, oil system, main bearing castings and oil sump designs. However, the Type 912 resembles the Type 907 2-litre engine in many important ways, and many castings and other components were carried forward.

For Lotus' own use, there was no immediate requirement for more peak horsepower, but there was certainly need for more torque, more evenly spread through the range, and any advance in fuel efficiency was to be welcomed. In addition, when the engine was being developed, it was expected that it would eventually be fitted to US-market Lotuses; however, as I explain in the last section of this chapter, this plan was never fulfilled.

After a great deal of work, therefore, the 2.2-litre engine was released for production with the same peak power output as before, but with much improved torque. A direct comparison between the three types of engine is as follows:

Engine   Peak power at rpm   Peak torque at rpm
Type 907, 1,973cc 160bhp at 6,200rpm 140lb/ft at 4,900rpm
Type 911, 2,174cc 150bhp at 5,750rpm 150lb/ft at 4,500rpm (Sunbeam-Lotus)
Type 912, 2,174cc 160bhp at 6,500rpm 160lb/ft at 5,000rpm (S2.2 Lotus)

It was also significant that the new Type 912 engine, for Lotus, developed 140lb/ft of torque (the old Type 907's peak figure) at a mere 2,400rpm, which serves to indicate how much more 'broad shouldered' and flexible the larger-capacity unit had become.

The new engine, in normally-aspirated form, and the models which had been developed to accept it, were announced in May 1980, even though the sensational turbocharged version, for the Essex Commemorative Turbo Esprit, had already been shown in February 1980, months before that car was ready to go on sale; this project is described in detail in Chapter 7. To emphasize the family nature of their latest cars, and the fact that all three had evolved in concert, Lotus elected to call each of the new models an S2.2 — Elite S2.2, Eclat S2.2 and Esprit S2.2.

At the same time they decided to drop the complex (and

In the autumn of 1981, Lotus added temporary interest to the front-engined models by introducing Riviera derivatives, which were mainly distinguished by the use of a lift-out sun-roof.

A feature of every Elite built from 1974 to 1983 has been the single, stubby, rear window wiper, whose pivot is actually in the glass itself.

confusing) way of identifying sub-derivatives, depending on whether they were fitted with such major items as power-assisted steering, air conditioning, or automatic transmission. Henceforth, there would only be one basic model of each type, and a long list of all the optional equipment could be specified by the customer or dealer at the time of ordering the car.

So as to avoid confusing the reader, I will split the descriptions of the front-engined S2.2s from that of the S2.2 Esprit:

Elite S2.2 and Eclat S2.2

Almost as important as any mechanical innovation was the fact that both the new front-engined Lotuses were significantly more expensive than their predecessors. The Elite S2.2 was priced at £16,142 (£732 more than the Type 501), and the Eclat S2.2 at £15,842 (which was no less than £1,140 higher than the Type 521). Taken on their own, these increases were not frightening, but it was one more step towards over-pricing in a falling market, which Lotus would have to deal with in the next year or so.

The instrument layout and switchgear of the Elite S2.2, announced in 1980, which nevertheless retained the same basic facia mouldings and simple two-spoke steering wheel.

Although the activities of Team Lotus were quite separate from those of Lotus Cars, the road-car company were always happy to remind the world of the racing team's successes. This body badge was added after Mario Andretti and his Lotus 79 had won the World Championship in 1978, and the marque Lotus had once again captured the constructors' crown.

Mechanically, the changes applied to both front-engined cars were effectively the same. Although the chassis design was not changed, the frame itself was now treated to a hot-dipped zinc coating, after the various pressings and foldings had been welded together. This galvanizing process endowed the backbone with truly enviable long-life prospects.

The suspension and steering of the cars was virtually unchanged, except that on the Eclat a new type of road wheel, with a 7in rim, was standardized — this was the same Speedline component as fitted to the front of Esprit S2s (and S2.2s). Rear braking was still by drums, and still inboard, while the fixed-length drive-shaft type of rear suspension was retained.

There was no longer a basic Eclat, which meant that pressed-steel road wheels and a four-speed gearbox no longer figured in the specification, even as an option.

The Type 912 2.2-litre engine was to the standard specification which I have already described, but behind it there was a completely different gearbox — a five-speed German Getrag, rather than Lotus' own transmission. Mike Kimberley and his management team had finally decided that, although it was nice to be able to offer a special-to-Lotus transmission, it was no longer financially viable, for in 1979 (for instance) a mere 557 front-engined Lotus cars with such a transmission had been built.

Several gearboxes had been assessed during development of new Lotus models before the Getrag design was chosen. This component was available with several different sets of ratios, and was already in use on other European road cars, notably the Vauxhall Chevette HS and Opel Ascona 400 'homologation specials', and on several different types of BMW saloon. Lotus chose ratios very similar to those of their own discarded transmission, and standardized a final-drive ratio of 4.1:1 (with a higher ratio of 3.73:1 available as an option). Once again, Borg-Warner three-speed automatic transmission was available as an option, for a mere £260 extra, but demand was still very low — a Lotus, somehow, just wasn't the sort of car people wanted to drive with automatic transmission. When the time came for the Eclat to be replaced by the Excel, the automatic option was discontinued.

Bodily, there were few obvious changes, but much detail work had been done. The front under-bumper spoiler was now neatly styled into the overall shape (Esprit S2-fashion), and different door under-sills reflected this slight change of style. The operation of the flip-up headlamp pods was now controlled by electric motors instead of by vacuum (so there was no longer any chance

If you didn't know that this was the central switch panel of the Elite S2.2, the decal would remind you. The position of the radio, behind the gear-lever, leaves much to be desired.

Neat but informative badging for the hatchback of the Elite S2.2.

Different trim and decoration was provided for the 2.2-litre-engined Elite, but the general layout was the same as before.

of leaking vacuum controls producing a salacious 'one-eye wink' from a modern Lotus!), and the new rear bumper included Rover SD1-style lamp clusters, as already used by the Esprits. Among many less obvious changes, the Elite's hatchback had been given an exterior lockable catch, and the tailgate wiper was now mounted in the tailgate glass.

There were interior revisions, mainly to seat styles and trim details, though the basic instrument and control layout was the same as it had been since 1974. There were new front seats, different seat tilt triggers and seat belts and rearranged facia details.

By the time the new cars went on sale — in May 1980, some

I'm glad the Elite S2.2 had good rear-view exterior mirrors, because the view out of the back window/hatch-back was restricted, to say the least. The rear seats have to be that shape, of course, because of the depth of the backbone frame.

weeks after the first production cars had been built — the market for such high-performance/high-price status cars had taken a nose-dive as Britain slipped into a deep recession. Two statistics tell their own story. In 1979, 230 Elites and 232 Eclats were built for British customers, and in 1980 these figures plunged to 99 and 95, respectively. The situation was to become even more critical in 1981, when a mere 12 Elites and 25 Eclats went to British buyers.

Part of the problem, Lotus now admit, is that their prices had risen beyond the level of their competitors', and hard-pressed entrepreneurial customers were reacting accordingly. Even though the S2.2 models were better, more flexible and altogether more reliable machines than the original versions of the Elite and

Eclat, they cost a great deal of money at a time when money was becoming increasingly scarce. The fact that the Elite was so good a car that it had been awarded the Don Safety Trophy was of no assistance.

The company claims that it was always aware of cost problems, because of the limited range (and, therefore, volume) it could offer, and because of the specialized nature of its cars. After all, if Colin Chapman was determined that Lotus should build as much as possible of its own cars (the figure of 70 per cent, by value, being approached during the late 1970s) at a volume of less than 1,000 cars a year, the cost consequences were clear. Mike Kimberley admits that at one time the company was doodling with a new M80

This low-level view of the nose of the S2.2 Eclat of 1980 shows how the detail styling of the spoiler, the bumper, the headlamps and the numberplate was achieved so elegantly.

Twin exhaust tail-pipes, Rover 3500 tail-lamps and a new set of decals identify the rear of an Eclat S2.2.

Should I really call this a Series 2, or an S2.2 Eclat? No matter — both types of decal were in evidence on the side of the larger-engined 2+2 fastback of 1980.

project, which was to have been a full four-door, four-seater model with the V8 engine, but that it never progressed beyond the mock-up stage. It is also admitted that from time to time Lotus considered buying-in proprietary engines to save money, and that apart from one obvious prime target, the 2.8-litre fuel-injected Ford Cologne V6 unit, there were investigations into American, French (PRV V6) and another British engine, but they all foundered when the long-term question of Lotus' image was measured up against these.

The crunch came in the autumn of 1981, at about the time the 20,000th 16-valve engine was built, and when the Riviera derivative was due for launch. Sales in the UK had virtually dried up, which was perhaps not surprising when the Elite S2.2 was priced at £17,206 and the Eclat S2.2 cost £16,751.

The company then took the bold decision to cut their prices substantially, partly by slashing their own ex-factory-gate margins, and partly by persuading dealers to trim their own mark-ups. From October 21, 1981, the Eclat price was chopped

by £1,894, and from January 1, 1982, the Elite's price was reduced by £1,616. When these reductions were noted alongside the lower price of the Esprit S3 (see below), the effect was quite marked. Even though the Elite had virtually disappeared from Hethel's production lines (14 built in 1982 compared with 13 in 1981), the Eclat bounced back from 31 to 91 sales.

In the meantime, Lotus had shown the Riviera version of both cars at the London Motorfair in October 1981. Mechanically these cars were not changed, the attraction being the lift-out sun-roof, for which an extra £405 was asked. It was the last important change made to these cars, for in October 1982 the first fruits of a liaison with Toyota would emerge, when the Eclat Excel would replace the Eclat S2.2 (see Chapter 8).

Esprit S2.2 and Esprit S3
At the same time as the front-engined S2.2 cars were announced, the Esprit S2.2 also made its bow. Since the Esprit had been updated as recently as August 1978, the differences between S2

The 2.2-litre Eclat of 1980, with interior trimmed in high-quality cloth.

Migraine sufferers might flinch away from the stripey styling of the 2.2-litre Eclat's seats. There was marginally better visibility out of the fastback's rear window and through the rear quarters than in the equivalent Elite.

As with the Elite, there was a Riviera derivative of the Eclat in 1981 and 1982.

If you ordered a sun-roofed Riviera, you were also given a badge on the tail to announce the difference to the world.

and S2.2 were limited to the use of a galvanized chassis treatment and the fitment of the Type 912 2.2-litre engine and a revised (partly stainless-steel) exhaust system. The price of the last S2 Esprit in Britain was £14,884, and that of the first S2.2 Esprit was £14,951 — a truly marginal increase. By the time it was withdrawn, in favour of the S3 Esprit, less than a year later, that price had risen to £15,270. The S3 model, however, was a very different animal indeed.

I can best summarize the new features included in the S3 by quoting Lotus' own press material: 'The Esprit Series 3 specification enabled us to rationalize a great many of the components, construction techniques and body/chassis tooling already incorporated in the Turbo Esprit . . . (we now produce 76 per cent of the motor car at Hethel).'

Because the new chassis-frame and suspension systems were

That charismatic moment which every factory visitor likes to see — the point at which a Lotus bodyshell is mated to the rolling chassis. This is a Series 2 Esprit on the simple production line at Hethel, now dismantled.

As announced, the Series 2 Esprit had a facia and interior to this style, retaining the two-spoke Elite/Eclat-type wheel, and now with BL Princess-type slide switches in the pod.

first seen in the Turbo Esprit, I describe them fully in the next chapter. The S3 Esprit, launched in April 1981, used the same rigid, backbone chassis-frame, revised rear suspension and modified front suspension, together with the larger disc brakes, as the Turbo Esprit, and it was also available with the 15in diameter Turbo Esprit wheels and tyres as an option. The bodyshell modifications introduced for the Turbo Esprit — larger front and rear bumpers (the rear bumper with the word 'Lotus' embossed into it), and new-style engine bay air intakes behind the rear quarter windows — were also standardized, though the Turbo's spoilers and side skirts were *not* offered (not even to customers

waving wads of pound notes or dollar bills!). A minor style change, which made a great deal of difference to the car's appearance, was that the lower sill and front spoiler mouldings were painted in body colour, rather than in black.

Mechanically, the S3 used the same engine and transmission as the deposed S2.2, so the performance was unaffected. Drivers, however, would probably notice a different (Turbo-type) steering wheel and some trim and sound-insulation improvements.

More important than all these changes, welcome though they were, was the considerably reduced price of the Esprit. Here was a real bargain, for the S3 was not only a better car than the S2.2 it

There was also a 1978 'World Championship Commemorative' Esprit S2 with a Momo steering wheel and leather trim facings, plus other detail differences.

replaced, but a cheaper car as well. The S2.2's final price was £15,270, while that of the first S3 was a mere £13,461. That reduction of £1,809, or nearly 12 per cent, made a lot of people sit up and take notice. It also did great things for the demand for Esprits, most of which were being sold in the UK; in 1980, 55 S2.2s had been produced for the UK market, while in 1981 there were 20 S2.2s and no fewer than 132 of the new S3s.

With the introduction of the S3 derivative, the Esprit 'came of age' and I can do no better than quote *Motor* in their test in August 1981: 'With a great many modifications aimed not only at reducing production costs but also at improving quality, it is a much better product all round, and a testament to Lotus' development abilities . . .'

What was interesting about the Esprit S3 was not what it had,

but rather what it did not have. For example, its drag coefficient was creditable at 0.33, but not sensational. As a Lotus engineer once told me: 'We never shouted about such things. In the early 1970s, even, we had C_d figures like that, and now other people are shouting about C_ds of 0.35. We don't spend millions on advertising — we just build efficient cars.'

It is also quite remarkable that the 135mph Esprit S3 does not have ventilated disc brakes. Ridiculous, you may say — every high performance car has ventilated discs. But not Lotus. The engineers at Hethel looked long and hard at their braking requirements, especially when the 150mph-plus Turbo Esprit was being developed; they tested solid and ventilated disc brakes and concluded that the solid discs gave them better results over a longer period. In the past Lotus cars may have had quality and

Compared with the original Esprit production car, the Esprit S2 had a different front spoiler and rear underbody profile, black plastic 'ears' behind the quarter windows, new wheels, and — of course — a distinctive set of decals to announce itself.

There were air intakes at each side of the car on the Esprit S2, just behind the side windows, to help channel cold air into the engine bay. As with other 1970s Lotus road cars, there were fuel fillers on each side of the car, too.

The S2.2 Esprit replaced the S2 model in 1980 at the same time as the engine was introduced for the front-engined cars, and it was visually unchanged except for new badging. Under the skin, apart from the enlarged engine, the big step forward was the incorporation of the galvanized chassis-frame.

Spot the differences? Only the badging on the rear quarters gives the game away — that this is the 2.2-litre-engined Esprit.

As the magazines used to say: 'The view most likely to be seen by other motorists' — the back of the Esprit, before it accelerated away into the distance. This was the 1980 S2.2, complete with updated 'World Championship' badges on the engine lid.

reliability shortcomings, but they could rarely be criticized on the grounds of engineering incompetence.

The Esprit S3 did not owe its splendid roadholding to exotic and expensive tyres such as the Pirelli P7, which are often found on Italian Supercars and can be extremely expensive to repair after a puncture. Instead, the S3 and the Turbo are equipped with Goodyear NCTs, which are more conventionally engineered, but still extremely grippy in all conditions. Neither does it cost a small fortune to have a punctured NCT mended — I know, for it has happened to me, with one of my own cars.

In 1983, Lotus announced the latest variation on the Esprit theme to coincide with their re-entry into the large US car market. Although the basis of the design was the successful S3 model, so much effort had gone into improvements to the bodyshell, the

For the Esprit Series 3 of 1981, many minor, but important, improvements were made to the style, including the use of different sill shapes, an all-over body colour (instead of black sills), more wrap-around bumpers, less prominent 'ears' and different wheels. The decals have changed, too!

On this Esprit S3 publicity car, the wheels are the optional BBS-type alloys normally fitted to the Turbo derivative. The word 'LOTUS' was embossed into a revised back bumper.

83

The driving controls of the Series 3 Esprit were much as before, except that the two-spoke Momo wheel was now standard and the trim style had changed yet again. Like all Esprits, the handbrake of the Series 3 car lived in the door sill, just ahead of the seat.

The Type 912 engine, of 2.2 litres capacity, was fitted to all Lotus road cars by the summer of 1980. Although considerably changed internally, from the outside it looked much the same as before.

provision of more space inside the cockpit, and tailoring the car to meet every US-market requirement, that the new Chairman, Fred Bushell, claimed that it was virtually another new model. Because of this, Lotus felt justified in calling the Federal car an S4.

During the 1970s, however, Lotus' involvement in the North American scene was not always happy or successful, and the entire range was withdrawn before any 2.2-litre-engined cars could be put on sale over there. To explain this, and to analyse the problems Lotus now admit to have encountered, I have prepared the extra section which follows.

Exports to the USA — the distribution saga
It is no exaggeration to suggest that Lotus' experience in selling cars to North America has often been disastrous. The United States is the richest potential car market in the world, recession or no recession, and Lotus' failure to establish a thriving market there with cars like the Eclat and Esprit was a real commercial tragedy. It is widely known that Lotus enjoyed a rush of sales in 1977 and 1978 and that sales collapsed immediately afterwards,

Spot the differences? The engine with twin Dellorto carburettors is for UK or 'Rest of the World' use, while that fitted with twin Zenith-Strombergs is for the USA, or perhaps Japan.

but it is not widely known why and how this happened.

On the face of it, any of the 16-valve-engined Lotus models should have found a ready market in North America. In engineering terms, there was no reason why the Lotus should be any less successful than cars like the mid-engined V6 and V8 Ferraris. For a short time, in fact, it all looked very promising, but then everything seemed to go wrong. Why?

To summarize the story, I have prepared a table from figures provided by Lotus. Unfortunately, production statistics for Federal cars also include those cars destined for Japan, where similar specifications apply; however, I know that the last front-engined cars for the USA were built in August 1980, and the last Esprits in February 1980. That said, the table tells its own story:

Lotus production — Federal-specification* cars

Model	1974	1975	1976	1977	1978	1979	1980	1981	1982	Total
Elite S1	42	141	80	34	17	19	20	—	—	353
Eclat S1	—	3	106	125	68	17	20	—	—	339
Esprit S1	—	—	4	474	—	—	—	—	—	478
Esprit S2	—	—	—	—	251	128	13	8	—	400
Esprit Turbo	—	—	—	—	—	—	—	9	3	12
Total	42	144	190	633	336	164	53	17	3	1,582

* Includes cars for Japan

John Lamm, writing in *Road & Track* in February 1983, had this to say:

'When Lotus updated its car line and image with the new Elite in 1974, and the Eclat and mid-engined Esprit a year later, it seemed the company was ready to continue offering the sort of automobiles we like: light, efficient, quick. And yet Lotus managed to fumble away what promised to be one of its best markets in the world, not because it lacked the right products, but because it couldn't build and distribute them for the US with anything like the brilliance that got the cars into production in the first place . . . It's my suspicion that Lotus has just about used up all its credit with automotive enthusiasts in the US. It hasn't been an easy account to deplete.'

When North American sales of these cars began in 1974, Lotus models were sold through a series of private distributors, with no centralized marketing and little forward planning. Lotus had great ambitions, however, and when one distributor suggested organizing national distribution to look after warranty, advertising, field service and sales, Lotus welcomed him, and Lotus Cars of America was set up.

Lotus engines were never simple, as this 2.2-litre Type 912 unit, in de-toxed form, makes clear. But it could be a lot more complicated — there is no air-conditioning pump or power steering fitted to this unit!

The Riviera Elites and Eclats were fitted with this type of lift-out roof section, for which £404.89 was asked.

In case other motorists had not noticed the special roof on Riviera derivatives, there was this rear corner decal to remind them.

But as Mike Kimberley told me: 'After 18 months, it was found that the organization had simply run out of money. In 1978-79 we were faced with seeing the market collapse by defaulting the customer on warranty costs, or we had to move in ourselves.'

As the 1979 Company Report then said:

'At the commencement of the year, we terminated our previous arrangements . . . and set up our distribution operation. . .'

The new company was Lotus North America Inc, based at Costa Mesa, in California, with a total staff of *nine* people, but it soon became apparent that the operation was far too small to cover such a vast continent. More people and more money were required, and Lotus could not provide either. Between 1977 and 1979, the output of Federal-specification cars mirrored the problem — 633 cars in 1977, 336 in 1978 and 164 in 1979.

It was at this juncture, when Lotus were agonizing over the imminent birth of the Esprit Turbo and the introduction of the 2.2-litre cars described above, that negotiations got under way with Rolls-Royce:

'David Plastow saw Colin and myself', Mike Kimberley recalls, 'and we came up with the idea of merging our US operations.' It

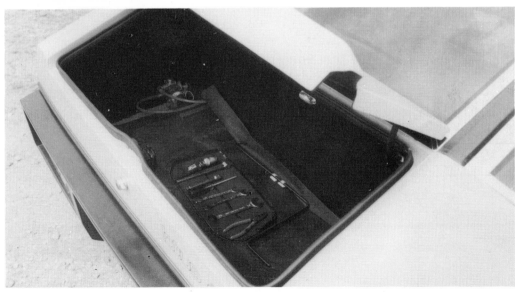

Not much room in the boot of an Eclat. The fuel pump lives on the left, and those are the standard tool roll and jacking handle as supplied by the factory.

was not so much a marketing merger as a takeover of Lotus' North American interests by Rolls-Royce, who already had an immensely well-organized, well-staffed business which had recently moved into new headquarters. A useful bonus was that this would work wonders for the 'Fleet Average' CAFE ratings of the Rolls-Royce and a very low overhead for Lotus. This five-year deal was announced by both companies in September 1979, when it was pointed out that Rolls-Royce Inc had 68 USA dealers, all of whom would handle Lotus sales.

Almost at once, however, things began to go wrong. As Mike Kimberley says: 'Rolls-Royce took over the cars which we already had in North America and ordered another 125, then the car market in the USA died — and died in a big way. Rolls-Royce had their own problems because of that, for in 1979-80 the £/$ exchange rate moved against us by 42 per cent, which was appalling. The nett result was that our dollar prices had to go shooting up, orders disappeared, and the distributors ordered no more cars from us. It's only fair to say that they had their own particular problems, with the Silver Spirit being announced —

perhaps that was quite enough, without having to bother with Lotus.'

The result was that Lotus sales plummeted still further, and when the changeover from 2-litre to 2.2-litre cars was made, exports from Hethel dried up altogether. This explains why no S2.2 Elites, S2.2 Eclats, or Esprit S2.2, S3 and Turbo models were officially sent to the North American market after that.

Both companies realized that the tie-up had failed and before the end of 1981 they began to negotiate closure, and the unscrambling of a complicated situation; a public announcement followed in summer 1982, but all loose ends were not tied up until early 1983.

The result was that Lotus' North American reputation was now in tatters, and no cars were sent there in 1981 and 1982. It looks, however, as if there may be yet another chapter in this story, for even as this book was being written a new business had been set up, and 'Federalized' Esprit Turbos were on their way to the United States. The details of this venture are discussed in the next chapter.

CHAPTER 7

Turbo Esprit

The 2.2-litre Supercar

Make no mistake, the Turbo Esprit is not just a slightly modified Esprit, and not just an easy and conventional way of gaining incremental sales for Lotus. In the scheme of things at Hethel it is very important, and technically very significant, if only for the fact that it was chosen to spearhead a new assault on the United States market in 1983.

I am tempted to suggest that if only Lotus had been able to give the car a different body style, they would certainly have been justified in giving it an entirely different name as well. Under the skin, which was extensively retouched by Giugiaro, there was a new chassis-frame, new rear suspension, new aerodynamic features and a turbocharged version of the 2.2-litre 16-valve engine, which produced no less than 210bhp. For this amazing car, Lotus claimed a top speed of 152mph — and it meant that they had produced their first true Supercar.

By any engineering standards, the Turbo Esprit was, and is, a phenomenal motor car. However, like the original Esprit, it was first shown to the public a long time before deliveries could possibly begin. The occasion of the car's launch was an extravagant party at the Albert Hall, in London, hosted by Team Lotus' Grand Prix sponsors at that time, Essex Petroleum, in which one of the three prototypes was displayed in the dramatic Essex blue, silver and red livery.

Although the Turbo Esprit was the first Lotus actually to be exhibited with a 2.2-litre engine, the normally-aspirated version of this unit had already gone into production for the S2.2 models. Even so, because of the rush to show a Turbo Esprit at the Albert Hall, the planned release of non-turbocharged engines was overshadowed for several months.

Lotus' own press material stresses the scope and nature of the new car's development: '. . . this new addition to our model range is not an Esprit with a bolt-on Turbo pack, but a fully developed and redesigned motor car in its own right.' So much of the car was new, indeed, that it would probably be easier to list what was *not* changed, modified, or improved. For a start, there was a new design of backbone frame, prepared not only because Lotus wanted to provide an altogether more integrated structure than before, and to accommodate a new rear suspension, but also because they wanted to leave enough space for the still-secret V8 unit to be fitted one day. Lotus now make no secret of the existence of a large-capacity V8 engine in their development programme, which explains why the engine bay of the new frame was altogether wider than before, and the general layout so much more sturdy.

At the front of the car, the independent front suspension (now with more Lotus-sourced parts than ever before) and rack-and-pinion steering of existing Esprits was retained, but at the rear there was a new layout. Earlier cars had used the simplest possible linkage, in which the fixed-length drive-shafts doubled as upper transverse links. The disadvantage of this was that cornering stresses were fed into the final-drive housing, found their way to the rest of the engine/transmission assembly, and did little to minimize harshness and vibration in the structure. For the new car, there was a new linkage, with a wide-based lower wishbone and an upper transverse link, which allowed the drive-shaft to have sliding joints and to carry out only one function; coil spring/damper units, of course, were also retained.

Development of the new car began before the end of 1977, and

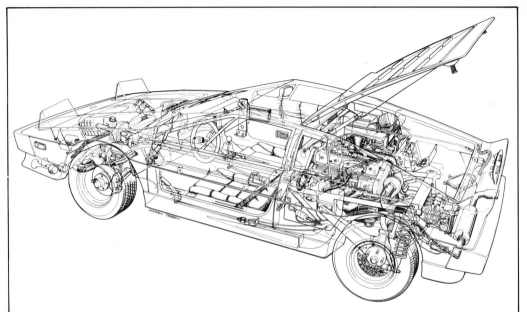

Andrew Dibben's excellent cutaway drawing of the Esprit Turbo, in left-hand-drive form, shows off the neat packaging of this exciting mid-engined model. There is not an ounce of wasted weight, or an inch of wasted space.

The schematic installation of the turbocharger to the 2.2-litre Lotus engine. In fact the turbocharger itself is not on top of the engine, but immediately behind it, above the clutch bellhousing.

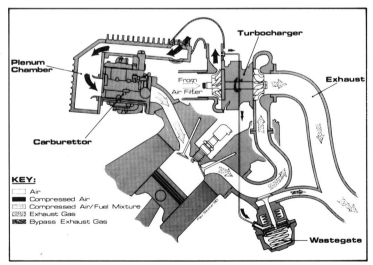

KEY:

- ☐ Air
- ■ Compressed Air
- ▨ Compressed Air/Fuel Mixture
- ▨ Exhaust Gas
- ▨ Bypass Exhaust Gas

if so much effort had not needed to be diverted into the De Lorean project, it would certainly have been announced months earlier than was the case. Even so, the M72, as the Turbo Esprit was known (M71 was the project including the V8 engine, by the way), progressed from 'good idea' to production car in little over two years. Apart from the new chassis and suspension, early decisions had to be made about the body style and the changes to the engine.

Compared with the bodyshell on normal Esprits of the period, there were many obvious changes and additions, mostly made for good aerodynamic reasons. The main shape and structure was unchanged, but differences were obvious from all angles. At the front, there was a larger wrap-round bumper, allied to a deep new spoiler. There were matching skirts along the sides, under the doors, complete with NACA-type ducts moulded in to direct cooling air towards the engine compartment.

At the rear there was a sizable and completely functional spoiler above the tail-lamps and number-plate, a large bumper matching the front component, and extra skirting under the tail. Above the

The complete Esprit Turbo engine/ transmission assembly, showing the complex cast exhaust system leading to the turbocharger, which is mounted above the clutch bellhousing, and the inlet trunking at the top of the unit. The Citroen SM-type gearbox is unchanged from the normal Esprit installation. The all-important wastegate control is low down, under the exhaust trunking, close to the turbocharger.

The carburation side of the Esprit Turbo engine/transmission shows virtually no evidence of turbocharging at all, except that the intake trunking to the carburettors is obviously different (and the word 'Turbo' is cast into the ribbed passage).

engine bay, instead of glass there was Venetian-blind style black louvring. In addition, not only to make the styling even more distinctive, but to optimize the roadholding, there were 15in diameter alloy road wheels of a new style, with 7in front and 8in rear rims and Goodyear NCT tyres. Most Turbos have been sold on BBS wheels, but a few early cars were supplied with three-piece Compomotive rims instead.

To produce the new Type 910 engine Lotus redesigned the Type 907 from end to end, and the final product differs in almost every detail from normally-aspirated Type 911 (Talbot Sunbeam-Lotus) and Type 912 (S2.2 Lotus) units. The finalized engine had its Garrett AiResearch turbocharger mounted above the clutch bellhousing, behind the cylinder block, and boosted inlet air to the Dellorto carburettors to a peak of 8psi above atmospheric pressure. To compensate for this, and to optimize all settings, the nominal compression was reduced to 7.5:1 (from 9.4:1) and there was a different camshaft profile. A feature not always noticed by the pundits was the dry-sump lubrication system, still not adopted on any other 16-valve Lotus car.

The result of a great deal of development work was not only a very powerful engine — peak power was 210bhp (DIN) at 6,250rpm and peak torque 200lb/ft at 4,500rpm — but one which was extremely flexible, having mostly 'non-turbo' habits. Its behaviour was so unexpectedly good, for instance, that *Motor Sport* headlined its test 'The perfect driving machine?', while *Autocar* called the very same car a 'Paragon of the turbocharged'. To deal with all this power, the only important changes were to the clutch (whose diameter was increased by an inch) and the brakes, which were larger — but not ventilated — at front and rear.

Inside the car, it was still the same basic layout as before, with no more space for stowing oddments, cases, or especially children(!), though there was a new and plushy type of trim and padding, while the Essex cars were given air conditioning as standard, and a complex Panasonic radio cassette player mounted in the centre of the roof panel; unfortunately this was FM (VHF wavelength) only, so was not liked by most customers and was dropped when the Essex Commemorative run was complete.

Although the Essex Turbo Esprit, price £20,950, had been announced in February 1980, deliveries did not begin until

When Renault racing engine designers visited Lotus to finalize their GP contract they looked around the factory. One of their designers inspected the Esprit Turbo engine, looked at the ribbed cast-alloy air passage from the turbocharger to the carburettors, and exclaimed: 'Ah yes, your intercooler!'. Not specifically intended to be so, the passage nevertheless has intercooling properties.

The rolling chassis of the Esprit Turbo, showing that the 210bhp engine takes up virtually no more space than the ordinary unit.

When covered by bodywork, the Esprit Turbo presents a bonnetful of engine to the enthusiast. On this model only, special camshaft covers are used, so that the 'Lotus' name is facing directly upwards.

August 1980, immediately after the summer holiday shut-down. However, although development work had been completed to 'Federalize' the sensational engine, the Turbo Esprit was not sent to the United States at this stage, for reasons which I have already explained. In its first calendar year, 1980, therefore, a total of 57 Turbos were built, of which 44 stayed in the UK.

Apart from the price of the Turbo — which in January 1981 had not changed from the launch figure — another feature which seemed to disturb some potential customers was the flamboyant Essex colour scheme. Very wisely, therefore, Lotus decided to offer a more conventional machine once the intended 100 'Essex' cars had been built. From April 1981 a Turbo Esprit in conventional colours, but still with all the appropriate body panels and decals, was made available for £16,917, though part of this whopping price reduction was due to the fact that air conditioning was now an optional extra. Demand perked up almost at once, and in spite of the generally reduced level of Lotus sales in 1981 and 1982, Turbo production rose to 116 in 1981 and 205 in 1982. In 1982, the Turbo was the fastest-selling Lotus model, backed up by

First seen only on the Esprit Turbo, but now standardized on all mid-engined Esprit models, was this much modified galvanized chassis-frame. The extra space around the engine bay was provided not only to allow for the turbocharged 2.2-litre engine, but to make way for the 4-litre four-cam V8 unit which Lotus have now admitted they are developing for the mid-1980s. An Esprit Turbo is already a Supercar, so how should I define the possibilities of a 300-plus bhp V8!

The sensational Esprit Turbo, complete with Essex Petroleum colour scheme, made its bow early in 1980. The basic Esprit style was embellished with a deeper front spoiler and skirts along the sides, and the wheels, of course, were 15in diameter, with wider rims.

Anyone who was passed by an Essex Esprit Turbo should have recognized it by the slatting over the engine and the much larger spoiler. The larger wheels probably would have been more difficult to spot.

This side view of the 1980 Essex Esprit Turbo (of which 100 examples were made) emphasizes the extra aerodynamic features of the bodyshell, including the deeper front spoiler, the larger rear spoiler and the F1-type skirting along the sides. The NACA ducts immediately below and behind the doors help to direct extra air into the hot engine bay.

the normally-aspirated Esprit S3, of which 160 cars were built. The glamorous publicity occasioned by the use of Turbo Esprits in the James Bond film *For Your Eyes Only* did no harm at all!

The big breakthrough for the Turbo Esprit, however, may have come in 1983, for as this book was being written the first examples were arriving in the United States and advance orders looked very promising indeed. Previous importing companies had never marketed the Turbo Esprit, even though the engine had always promised to be outstandingly efficient in Federal guise.

Lotus had had several traumatic experiences in trying to sell and support cars in the United States, but now Mike Kimberley thinks a new deal is the best of all possible worlds. Before the end of 1982, a new company, Lotus Performance Cars LP, was set up on the East Coast, headed by John A. Spiech (previously General Manager of Ferrari, North America (a 1,000 cars per year

operation) and it was suggested that 350 cars would be sold in 1983, with 700 projected for 1986.

As Mike Kimberley told me: 'We have a special car for this market which is really a brand new model, with a new set of body moulds, a lot more space, foot boxes and headroom, and so on. We're going in for the first time ever with a clean market. There hasn't been a mid-engined Lotus for sale over there since 1981, and the Turbo was never launched over there, so it's all new.'

Even though the 1983 Federal Turbo Esprit kept its original project number of M72, it was new or modified in many respects, and factory personnel were very excited about its prospects, especially as the peak power output had needed only minor trimming. Lotus view the realignment of £/$ exchange rates as an unqualified bonus for them as exporters. Early in 1983 they were expecting to price their Turbo Esprit at $48,000, compared with

The squashy-looking interior of an early Esprit Turbo, with the basic instrument and control layout unchanged.

This complex-looking communications panel, by Panasonic, was only fitted to the Essex Esprit Turbos — it was attached to the inside of the roof panel, high above the transmission/services tunnel.

The Esprit Turbo looks just as smart without its Essex livery. This white example was parked in the centre of Norwich for a photocall. We hope the policeman is not about to book the car for a parking offence!

Prince Michael of Kent is a real motoring enthusiast, and he thoroughly enjoyed a demonstration drive in a JPS Esprit Turbo at Donington Park, with GP driver Nigel Mansell at the wheel.

the $60,000 asked for the equivalent two-seater Ferrari 308. 'And,' as Mike Kimberley quoted with glee, 'our car will do 0-60mph in 6.5 seconds, in full de-toxed trim, whereas that Ferrari takes 8.3 seconds.'

Since March 1983, all Turbo Esprits have been built with conventional wet-sump engine lubrication. The dry-sumping introduced in 1980 was always agreed to be a real safety-conscious 'belt and braces' job, and prolonged testing convinced the engineers that it was not really needed.

The success of this car, and the almost universal praise for its engineering, behaviour and detail fittings, all go to prove that at this price a customer is more interested in the right specification than he is in mundane practicality. If you are not in the Turbo Esprit price class, you simply would not appreciate that the extrovert good looks also have a functional effect on the car's aerodynamics, and you would no doubt complain about the limited space for stowage and the use of an SR-rated 14in get-you-home spare wheel. But if you were, you would not only know about the aerodynamics, but you would appreciate the inter-cooling effect of the finned manifolding from turbocharger

The front stowage compartment of the Esprit Turbo really has no space to accommodate anything except the proverbial toothbrush. The wheel is a small-diameter/speed-derated spare — merely a 'get you home' or 'get you to a garage' emergency fitting.

The Esprit Turbo facia layout, virtually the same as for the normal Esprit. The turbocharger boost gauge is in the centre of the instrument board between the speedometer and rev-counter, the layout (in 1980) being completely different from that of the current S2 Esprit.

Not to be confused with the factory machine, the Esprit Turbo produced by Bell & Colvill, the well-known British Lotus dealers, from Surrey, had entirely different carburation and trunking arrangements, as a conversion of normally-aspirated Esprits.

to carburettor plenum chamber, the remarkable grip and handling and the excellent lie-down driving position. And if you were a Turbo Esprit enthusiast, you would make sure that you never went kerb hopping to cause punctures anyway . . .

To avoid confusion in future years, I must mention the existence of the Bell & Colvill Esprit Turbo at this stage. Bell & Colvill, based at West Horsley in Surrey, are Lotus dealers, and in 1978 they announced their own privately-financed turbocharged conversion on the basis of the Esprit S2. This car, of course, was the 2-litre model, and the turbocharging layout was entirely different, having been developed by Stuart Mathieson on his own account. In this conversion, priced at £2,000, there was a single and very large SU carburettor upstream of the Garrett AiResearch turbocharger, which fed the fuel-air mixture at a maximum boost of 8psi to the engine, whose nominal compression ratio had been reduced to 7.5:1 by the use of new pistons. Peak power was quoted at 210bhp at 6,000rpm, while peak torque was 202lb/ft.

Although it was neither as flexible, nor as refined as the factory Turbo which was to follow, the Bell & Colvill car was undoubtedly very fast, with a top speed of more than 150mph claimed, 0-60mph in 6.2 seconds and 0-100mph in 17.2 seconds. The only way that one could identify this car externally was because B & C had added 'turbo' decals to the front and sides of the car, near the factory's own 'Esprit' decals.

Lotus, however, always appreciated that a proportion of their clientele liked their cars with something of a traditional layout, and with more than two seats. For them, the Elites and Eclats had been on sale since 1974 — but by the early 1980s their appeal was on the wane. Something had to be done about this — and the Lotus Excel of 1982 was the result.

CHAPTER 8

Excel

Applying the Toyota touch

By the beginning of 1981 the Lotus Group, and Colin Chapman himself, were overdue for a welcome boost to their fortunes, for the last couple of years had been traumatic in the extreme. Put in a nutshell, Lotus car production had dropped from 1,200 a year to a mere 383, and pre-tax profits had slumped from £1,283,000 to £461,000. Worse was to follow.

In Britain, a change of government in 1979 had been accompanied by rising inflation and a sharp but completely unjustified boost in the exchange rate of the pound sterling. All over the world, a recession, triggered off by the second great oil shock, was setting in. In North America, Lotus' marketing link-up with Rolls-Royce had clearly not been a success, for sales had virtually collapsed. At Hethel the only course was to cut back considerably on production of new cars, and unhappily to make some of the workforce redundant.

Lotus could not even look to the engineering contracting side of their business to bolster them up, for the massive development job for De Lorean was completed by the end of 1980, and production of Talbot Sunbeam-Lotus hatchbacks at Ludham was already past its peak, with the closure of Linwood (where these bodyshells were built) already being forecast for 1981. Even on the race tracks (while reminding ourselves that Team Lotus were almost completely divorced from the road car-building Lotus Cars) there was little to cheer up the firm, for the cars had not won a Grand Prix since 1978, and the controversial twin-chassis Lotus 88 being built for 1981 was soon to run into trouble from the legislators of the sport.

No matter. It was altogether typical of Colin Chapman, in his capacity as the long-term planning Chairman of the Group (with

Mike Kimberley running Lotus Cars for him, as that company's Managing Director) that he did not let this get him down. Chapman was still a fiercely independent character, who did not want to see his companies swallowed up by a larger combine. However, there was no doubt that Group Lotus found itself in a serious position, not only in financial terms, but also in the market place.

Many of the 'traditional' Lotus customers were becoming rather bored with the products, which had changed very little since 1975. The upgrading of all cars to 2.2-litres had not been accompanied by any styling improvements, and it was already becoming distressingly obvious that Lotus cars were now very expensive indeed, at a time when many typical Lotus buyers were cutting back on their spending to help ride out the recession.

It is always dangerous for an author to try to summarize a company's strategic decisions, especially when complete documentation cannot be made available, but the action taken in the first months appears to have been on three fronts — there would be price reductions (already discussed in previous chapters), work would start on a new generation of Lotus cars, not as direct replacements for the existing cars, and major changes would be investigated for the front-engined models.

Perhaps we will not be told for some years to come if Colin Chapman talked to many larger companies when he was formulating his future strategy. However, we *do* know that he eventually came to an agreement with Toyota of Japan, probably as a result of work which the company carried out on the Toyota Supra sports coupe. This is not the place to speculate too closely on the layout of the brand new Lotus which is known to be on the

The rear end of the Excel chassis shows off the new and more compact Toyota differential, the outboard rear disc brakes, the different bracing details and the latest suspension linkage.

The front of the Excel rolling chassis looks much as before, except that the experts would recognize the Toyota brakes. The Toyota Supra-based gearbox is hidden from view in this shot.

The decision to call the new car the
Excel was not taken until a late stage.
As these pictures show, the restyled
car was originally to have been called
an Eclat 3, for it was badged as such on
the nose . . .

. . . and on the tail.

The Excel has a nicely detailed nose-cum-bumper, with the spoiler and air intakes all neatly incorporated.

way, except to emphasize that this is a very important car for Lotus' future. The immediate effect on the link-up with Toyota, however, was the Lotus Excel, which made its bow in October 1982.

Perhaps it is over-simplifying the project a little, but I would describe this as a thorough reworking of the Eclat layout, with the object of using Toyota running gear wherever possible, and updating the styling, not only to freshen up the image, but to improve the car's aerodynamics. The new car is called the Eclat Excel, to emphasize the direct links with the past, even though much has changed under the skin. The work was completed at high speed — not merely the engineering design and development, but all the new tooling which was required. Specifically, the project was started in the spring of 1981, some weeks before Lotus made this announcement:

'Lotus Cars and Toyota Motors share the desire to co-operate on a long-term basis in engineering, manufacturing and other areas where practical. Following detail discussions on these subjects, agreement has been reached in principle between the two companies for future close co-operation and the supply of certain components.'

One important aim with the new car, which was called 'Eclat 3' for a time (I have reproduced pictures of a prototype badged as such), and was also given the project number of M55 (and, confusingly, Lotus 89, which had already appeared on a Formula 1 car of 1981!) was to reduce material costs without in any way degrading the specification.

There was never any question of abandoning the splendid 16-valve engine, which will be used in some Lotus models for years to come, though a new and more efficient exhaust system, with 40 per cent less back pressure, was specified. The gearbox, however, was different — and this made it the third gearbox to be used in successive models in less than three years.

Lotus had dropped their own BL/Beans five-speed unit in 1980, and all previous 2.2-litre front-engined Lotus cars had been fitted with the beefy Getrag five-speeder. Now this was displaced in favour of a Toyota transmission. Like previous boxes used in this Lotus layout, it had an overdrive fifth gear ratio and was basically the same as that fitted to the 2.8-litre/170bhp Toyota Celica Supra XX coupe. Compared with the original BL/Beans

The nose of the Excel is subtly different from that of the Eclat S2.2, which it displaced, in almost every way and there is no air outlet on the bonnet.

and Getrag transmissions, the internal ratios of the Toyota box are as follows:

Toyota type   0.78, 1.00, 1.27, 1.89, 3.28, reverse 3.77:1
Getrag type   0.81, 1.00, 1.39, 1.93, 2.96, reverse 3.70:1
BL/Beans type   0.80, 1.00, 1.37, 2.01, 3.20, reverse 3.46:1

Naturally the Toyota gearbox was amply robust for its job, and it was driven through the same 8.5in diaphragm spring clutch as the 2.2-litre Eclat, but it was lighter and more efficient, with lower transmission losses.

Matching it was the Supra XX's chassis-mounted final drive, which had a 4.1:1 ratio, but no limited-slip differential. Incidentally, one of the problems always experienced with the previous Salisbury final drive had been that individual units tended to be noisy, but the Toyota component was both quiet and impressively reliable.

Automatic transmission was not offered on the new car, even though there was a suitable overdrive four-speed automatic gearbox in the Toyota 'parts bin'. This transmission is available in Supras sold in the USA, but not in Britain, where, however, it is to be found in the Volvo 760GLE saloon.

Compared with the Eclat 2.2, the chassis was modified in many small ways and was galvanized, but the layout was the same as before, as was the wheelbase and the front track, but the rear suspension had been updated, rather after the fashion of the Esprit S3, which is to say that transverse top links were fitted to provide sideways location, and were allied to wide-based lower

Side aspect of the Excel should be compared with that of the final Eclats. Not only is the rear side window shape different, but so is the boot lid cut-off, the decoration behind the doors, the door handles (Toyota), the position of the fuel filler . . . the list is not quite endless, but extensive.

Definitive badging for the Excel which, strictly speaking, is an Eclat Excel.

The standard interior of the Excel, really very little different from the Elite/Eclat models of the 1970s. The steering wheel, as ever, was a two-spoke design . . .

. . . but as an extra one could have this 'Personal' wheel, which looked more stylish. Magazine road-testers seemed to prefer it, too.

wishbones, while the new drive-shafts (by Toyota, also from the Supra XX) had plunging universal joints, rather than being fixed in length.

There was also an important change in the braking system. All previous Elites and Eclats, built from 1974 to 1982, had been fitted with front wheel disc brakes and inboard-mounted rear drum brakes. For the Excel, however, there were Toyota discs at front and rear, ventilated instead of solid, and the rear discs were mounted outboard. In the modern manner, the handbrake operated on small drums mounted inside the hub of the rear discs. Naturally there was vacuum-servo assistance and split hydraulic circuits. As before, of course, there was rack-and-pinion steering, with optional power assistance which, in spring 1983, was priced at a whopping £650.33. The road wheels were the familiar Lotus/Speedline pattern, as used on the Eclat 2.2, with 7in wide rims and 205/60VR-14in Goodyear NCT tyres.

The most obvious changes were to the styling, which was still recognizably developed from that of the Eclat, but with many new and modified features. The first thing to emphasize is that no hatchback Elite version of the new chassis was ever proposed —

Like the earlier cars, the Excel had individual rear seats — which was quite unavoidable because of the depth of the backbone frame.

demand for this shape began to fade away in 1980, and by the time the Excel package was ready for launch the Elite was only being built to special order.

Glass-fibre technology at Lotus continues to improve in leaps and bounds (though at the time of writing the long-awaited injection of paint at the moulding stage has not been put into series production), so much so that the company no longer like to see their cars described as having GRP shells. The new word is 'Composite', and this should certainly be applied to the Excel's shell. The Lotus VARI system was retained, as was the use of RRIM mouldings for bumpers and sill panels, along with strengthening foam in certain box and stiffening sections.

So much was conventional, evolutionary Lotus. As to the style, there was a new and somehow softer nose outline, with no radiator air outlet on the top surface, the waistline (junction between body side panels and side glass) was different, as was the layout of the rear quarters. There was further evidence of Toyota 'parts bin' engineering in such matters as outside door handles, and the fuel filler cap was now masked by a cover decorated with a smart 'ACBC' Lotus badge.

The Excel's rolling chassis, complete with 5-speed Toyota (Supra-based) gearbox, final drive, disc brakes and other details. The frame is galvanized, of course.

Inside the car the layout was much as before, but a series of modifications in the back gave rear seat passengers more headroom than before; Lotus claimed 4in extra, but *Autocar's* road-test figures make it 1.5in. There was also an optional three-spoke Personal steering wheel for this car, but in general the majority of cars have so far been built with the familiar two-bar Lotus wheel.

The important feature of the new body style was that it was aerodynamically more efficient, for Lotus claimed a C_d figure of 0.32, which compared with the latest Eclat's C_d figure of 0.34.

This, it was claimed, added up to a 7 per cent improvement, and when a 6 per cent improvement in power transmitted to the road wheels was also taken into consideration, it meant that performance and fuel economy should both be improved.

The final and very important factor was the car's price. In October 1982, when the Excel was introduced, the price of the equivalent Eclat S2.2 was £14,896. The Excel cut this considerably, to £13,787, which was a saving of no less than £1,109. The commercial tie-up with Toyota was already beginning to pay off!

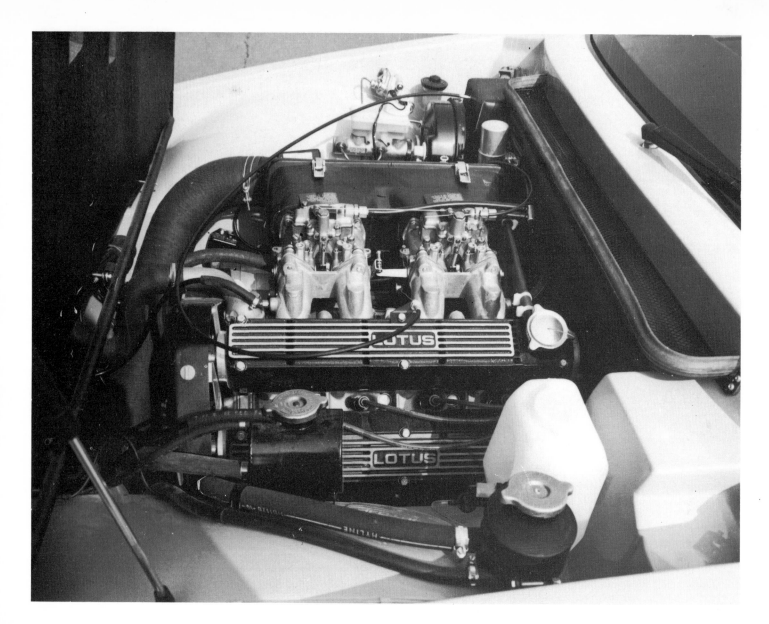

Two views of the 1983 Excel engine bay — with little evidence of the Toyota influence which was beginning to make itself felt.

The new car, at the new price, could not have arrived at a better time, for all kinds of negative comment was being made about Lotus in the wake of the De Lorean collapse. By the standards of late 1982, the Excel was seen to be a real bargain — after all, in the summer of 1981 the Eclat S2.2 had been priced at £16,262, reduced to £14,896 later that year, and now here was a better, more efficient and freshly styled car for a mere £13,787. In a year, the price of owning a 130mph front-engined Lotus had dropped by £2,475.

It almost goes without saying that Lotus enjoyed an extremely successful showing at the NEC in October 1982, after which they were able to announce that they had outstanding orders for 218 cars (of which 80 per cent were for Excels) and that the production line capacity was completely full up until the end of March 1983.

The first Excel, actually an export market car, had been built in September 1982, and by the end of the year a total of 71 Excels (all but two for the home market) had been manufactured. Every time I visited Hethel in the spring of 1983, in the course of gathering material for this book, the waiting list for new Excels was growing longer. The assembly shops were visibly filling up again, and it was not long before Lotus announced that they would certainly be building more than 800 cars in 1983. Since modern cars are becoming more complex and time-consuming to build than cars of a few years ago, it meant that Lotus Cars' road car activity was heading back towards 1979 levels, very rapidly indeed.

Road tests confirmed what Lotus claimed for the car. *Autocar*, who have tested every one of the front-engined Lotuses, found that it was faster in a straight line (130mph) and had more flashing acceleration (0-100mph in 20.1 seconds, for instance, and a standing-start quarter-mile in 15.4 seconds) than any previous ancestor. The fact that it was no more economical than before merely confirmed the way in which it was driven by every tester. They found that it handled wonderfully well and performed every function with geat aplomb. It was no wonder, then, that they summed it up as a 'Paragon of Poise', and in the text called it a 'completely different and dramatically improved car'.

Tragically, on December 16, 1982, just as Lotus was beginning to hum again, Colin Chapman died of a heart attack, and temporarily left the Group without a leader. It was a shattering blow to everyone connected with him, and caused great uneasiness in the business and financial communities. But Colin obviously left his spirit behind in the company, for in a matter of weeks it seemed to be forging ahead just as strongly as ever. The new Chairman, Fred Bushell, was able to announce not only that the outstanding loans to American Express had been paid off, but that new credit facilities had been arranged, a major expansion programme had been planned for the next three years and an entirely new M90 model would be introduced in 1985.

1981 and 1982 had been traumatic years, the 1981 financial year producing a pre-tax loss of £109,000 (the first Group loss since 1975) to be followed by a deeper deficit in the first half of 1982. On the other hand, there was evidence that the company was beginning to pull out of its own personal recession, and the indicators were mostly encouraging.

In that Lotus themselves had made public reference to the M90 project, I can also mention it here, if only to make clear that it is not to be another variation on the 1970s theme. As far as this book is concerned, I can say with confidence that the established range of Excel, Esprit and Esprit Turbo will be continued, in developed form, for some time to come. The M90, on the other hand, has been freely rumoured to be the 'Elan of the 1980s', and will certainly have a Toyota engine, not the famous Lotus 16-valve unit. Mike Kimberley has made it clear to me, as has the public pronouncement from Lotus, that he sees the M90 as being a car to restore real volume to Hethel: 'The factory has always been capable of producing 4,000 to 5,000 cars a year in terms of floor area. When we get the next new model we won't need any more bricks and mortar — our intention is to mechanize.' A major financial restructuring involving British Car Auctions and Toyota and approved in August 1983 was to make this possible.

This, however, is not the end of the story as far as the modern-engined Lotus cars are concerned for, during the 1970s and early 1980s, several other cars used the 16-valve engine. I must now devote some space to discussing these machines — and it would also be quite wrong of me to ignore the De Lorean project altogether.

CHAPTER 9

Jensen and Talbot

The Lotus engine users

This book would be incomplete if I did not relate the story of the two other cars which used the 16-valve Lotus engine in the 1970s and early 1980s — the Jensen-Healey and the Talbot Sunbeam-Lotus. Both were built in considerable numbers and, therefore, contributed materially to Lotus' financial health during an often-troubled period. Without the Jensen-Healey business, Lotus would have been financially over-stretched for a couple of years, when their new engine facility was ready, but the cars for which it was intended were not.

The Jensen-Healey had its origins in the 1960s and in the formation of British Leyland. Donald Healey had enjoyed a successful business relationship with BMC throughout the 1950s and 1960s in links involving the Austin-Healey marque, but once British Leyland, controlled by Sir Donald Stokes, came into being (of which the old BMC was just one part), it became clear that Healey was to be frozen out. Then and there, Donald and his son Geoffrey started to look around for a new opportunity.

The Austin-Healey 3000 (the 'Big Healey', as it was always affectionately known) had disappeared by 1968, so the Healeys began to talk to the California-based businessman, Kjell Qvale (who had garage businesses which had sold many Austin-Healeys) about a successor. In 1968, with little idea of where they would build a new car, they began to evolve a new two-seater sports car, styled originally by Hugo Poole, then modified by Bill Towns, which was to use Vauxhall Viva GT suspension and running gear.

In 1970, the opportunity came for Qvale (who was a rich man) to buy Jensen Motors, of West Bromwich, from the merchant bankers William Brandt. This was achieved in April 1970, whereupon Qvale installed Donald Healey as the company's new Chairman and instructed Jensen's Chief Engineer, Kevin Beattie, to take up the new project and productionize it as speedily as possible.

At this point the new car ran into trouble on two counts — the styling and the choice of engine. The style had to be modified to meet certain legislative requirements, and was later altered again to take account of Qvale's taste, the result being a rather anodyne open two-seater shape.

The engine problem was simple — at first. While the Vauxhall Viva GT unit was freely available to Jensen and Healey, it rapidly became clear that the ever-tightening US exhaust emission regulations would strike hard at its power capabilities. For 1972 it seemed certain that Jensen would end up with a gutless wonder.

The search was suddenly on at West Bromwich for alternative power and, with it, an alternative gearbox. Amazingly nobody seems to have approached Lotus at first, even though it was known that their engine had originally been built up on the same cylinder block as that used in the Vauxhall Viva GT. Colin Chapman, however, made the first approaches, but could only offer up to 60 engines a week (Jensen were planning to build up to 200 cars a week, 60 per cent of which would be destined for sale in North America).

In a great rush, therefore, Jensen investigated the German Ford V6 engine of the Capri RS2600, the 2-litre BMW four-cylinder unit, the Volvo four-cylinder and even the new Wankel rotary engine from Mazda. It was not long, however, before Chapman re-opened negotiations on behalf of Lotus when it became clear that the Elite would not be ready for at least a couple of years, which meant that he could supply much higher

Jensen were the first major users of the Type 907 engine, in the two-seater Jensen-Healey sports car. The Lotus connection was never advertised on the car's exterior.

quantities of the Type 907 engine to West Bromwich.

After Chapman and Fred Bushell had flown to California to finalize the deal with Kjell Qvale, the deed was done in the spring of 1971. It was officially revealed to the press in October 1971, with the forecast that Jensen would be taking up to 15,000 engines a year (or 300 a week — the quantities quoted were getting quite out of hand!) and that deliveries would begin early in 1972. The engine, it was stated, would be rated at 140bhp for Europe and 115bhp for the United States. As in the forthcoming Lotus installation, it would be installed at an angle of 45 degrees in the engine bay, leaning over towards the left side of the car.

The Jensen-Healey (for such was its name, there being no mention of Lotus) was launched in March 1972, in time for showing at the Geneva exhibition, and the first deliveries began soon afterwards. It was a neat but rather plain looking car, for which the drag coefficient was claimed to be 0.42. The Vauxhall

An early Jensen-Healey on test at Lotus, with the car stationary, but 'running' on the roller-rig chassis dynamometer. This particular car is in left-hand-drive, 'Federal' guise — and the Lotus engine has twin Zenith-Stromberg carburettors.

suspension and back axle had been retained, though the Lotus engine was backed by a non-overdrive Sunbeam Rapier four-speed all-synchromesh gearbox.

Deliveries began at a total British price of £1,811, which compared with £2,116 for the current Lotus Elan Sprint, and original road tests showed that the car had a top speed of nearly 120mph (which was achieved at 6,650rpm, just over the peak of the power curve), but that it was out-paced and out-handled by the less-powerful Elan. We did not know that Lotus would rate their own engine at 160bhp for the new-generation Lotus cars, and at the time we thought the 140bhp rating of the engine as supplied to Jensen, and the performance it produced, was quite satisfactory.

The story of the Jensen-Healey is easily told, for the car finally went out of production in the spring of 1976 when Kjell Qvale called in the Receiver to close down the unprofitable Jensen business. This was not really the fault of the Jensen-Healey (or the estate car-style Jensen GT, a sort of Elite copy, which arrived in 1975), though sales never approached the 15,000 a year once mentioned; it was that in the aftermath of the Suez war of 1973, the market for the big Chrysler-engined Jensen Interceptors faded away rapidly and dragged the company down into bankruptcy.

No major changes were made to the Lotus-supplied engine of the Jensen-Healey in the four years in which it was in production, though the Chrysler gearbox behind it was changed for a German

The 'Federal' Jensen-Healey, like later Lotus-used engines, had twin horizontal Zenith-Stromberg carburettors. In this illustration the cam drive belt cover is not yet fitted, though the unique-to-Jensen tubular exhaust manifold has been fitted.

Getrag box from November 1974. A total of 10,912 of these cars were built, and a breakdown of statistics is as follows:

Model analysis:	Jensen-Healey	10,453
	Jensen GT	459
Annual production: (Jensen-Healey)	1972	705
	1973	3,846
	1974	4,550
	1975	1,301
	1976	51
Deliveries by market: (Jensen-Healey)	Domestic	1,914
	USA/Federal	7,709
	Other export	830

Demand for the Jensen-Healey was already contracting before the company went into liquidation. There is no doubt, however, that the Jensen business was very valuable to Lotus, even though they were left with a large excess engine-building capacity in 1976 when the Jensen-Healey/Jensen GT model died.

The imbalance between Lotus engine production at its peak and at its lowest point is remarkable. In 1974, 4,550 Jensen-

Assembly of engines for the Jensen-Healey under way at Hethel. The lightweight, but very strong, cylinder block is much in evidence.

Healeys and 687 Lotus Elites were built — 5,237 cars in all. In 1977 total Lotus production was 1,070 of all types, and the Jensen business had been lost.

Lotus, no doubt, were delighted to be approached by Chrysler UK for engine supplies in 1978, especially when the company started talking about substantial numbers of engines. The amazing thing, however, is that the Chrysler Sunbeam-Lotus (which was renamed Talbot Sunbeam-Lotus almost as soon as it had been announced) was not a carefully researched and product-planned performance car, but the result of a brainwave by Des O'Dell, Chrysler's dynamic Director of Motorsport. It was only after O'Dell decided on a particular car layout which he considered ideal for rallying that he approached his management for backing.

At the end of 1977, Chrysler's 16-valve Avenger-BRM was outlawed from motor sport by a change in regulations, and O'Dell was looking around rather desperately for a new opportunity. For the basic 'chassis', he decided almost at once to use the Chrysler Sunbeam hatchback, which used a shortened version of the Avenger's floorpan and had a smart but simple three-door superstructure.

Jensen-Healey installation of the 2-litre Type 907 engine, complete with Dellorto carburettors and distinctively badged camshaft covers and featuring a large separate AC air cleaner in the engine bay, connected to the engine by flexible trunking.

The original Chrysler Sunbeam-Lotus of spring 1979, painted black and silver, with Lotus roundels on the car's flanks. By the time the car went on sale in the summer it had been rebadged as a Talbot.

117

Lotus supplied a 2.2-litre version of the 16-valve engine for the Chrysler/Talbot Sunbeam-Lotus, rated at 150bhp. Apart from the 'Chrysler' camshaft covers on this prototype (which reverted to standard 'Lotus' for production cars), and the special carburettor intake trunking, the engine looks very familiar to all Lotus enthusiasts.

There was nothing spartan about the facia and instrumentation of the Talbot Sunbeam-Lotus. There is no 'Lotus' badging in this style — but a driver surely didn't have to be told!

The problem was that a new and very powerful engine was needed to make the car competitive. At the time, the Ford Escort RS was completely dominant in international rallying, setting the standard with a 240-250bhp 2-litre engine, while the Vauxhall Chevette HS (which used some Lotus components, as I describe below) was almost as fast.

There was no way that Chrysler themselves could produce a competitive engine (time, money and design expertise were all lacking), so O'Dell looked around for a proprietary unit. It needed little investigation to show that the 16-valve Lotus engine was the only suitable one. Early in 1978, therefore, O'Dell acquired a rally-tuned Type 907 from Lotus, shoehorned it into a Sunbeam hatchback, matched it to a five-speed German ZF gearbox and a more robust back axle, and went testing. The 'motor industry grapevine' system worked well, for O'Dell's Development Engineer, Wynn Mitchell, had known Lotus' Mike Kimberley for years . . .

On the strength of one car, some test results and an outstanding (unhomologated) test debut on the Mille Pistes rally, when Tony Pond took second place, O'Dell got approval for a run of cars to

The Sunbeam-Lotus in its element — with a works car rallying on a variety of surfaces. This was Henri Toivonen and Paul White on their way to winning the 1980 Lombard-RAC Rally outright. Other works-supported cars took third and fourth places in the same event. The power output of a works car, with their own big-valve engine, was around 250bhp.

Works competition Sunbeam-Lotus cars under preparation at Coventry in 1981. With a total of only six cars, Talbot won the World Rally Championship for Makes in that season.

This is a Lotus publicity shot, of course, for no normal Sunbeam-Lotus was normally badged with 'Essex' on the doors. But was the hatchback *really* so much taller than the Esprit Turbo?

allow him to homologate the Chrysler Sunbeam-Lotus, as it was to be called. To get the car approved into FISA Group 4 (in which the Ford, Vauxhall, Fiat 131 Abarth and other Supercars were all placed), 400 would have to be built in less than a year. Chrysler, however, made hasty enquiries around their dealers and overseas concessionaires, and decided they could do much better than this — by the time the car was announced they had laid plans to build no fewer than 4,500 cars!

Between the decision to build the cars, which was taken in mid-1978, and the public launch of the machine in March 1979, there had also been a corporate upheaval, though this never affected the Sunbeam-Lotus' career. Chrysler of Detroit tired of sustaining losses in their European subsidiaries and sold out to the Peugeot Citroen group in September 1978. As part of the rationalization and realignment programme which followed, the British Chryslers of 1978 became Talbots from August 1979.

This car, in fact, was the first to use the enlarged, 2.2-litre Type 911 Lotus engine which, compared with the Type 912 fitted to S2.2 Lotuses, had different carburettor settings, ignition, lubrication system and main bearing castings, and a different oil sump to clear the front-suspension crossmember.

For the Talbot, the engine was rated at 150bhp (DIN) at 5,750rpm, while peak torque was 150lb/ft at 4,500rpm, which effectively put it half-way between the engines once supplied to Jensen and those used by Lotus themselves. In its class, of course, this made the Talbot Sunbeam-Lotus very competitive in road car form, for the limited-production Vauxhall Chevette HS had 135bhp, while the Ford Escort RS1800 (with 120bhp) had recently been dropped.

The five-speed ZF gearbox fitted to the Sunbeam-Lotus was certainly not as smooth, nor as refined as the Getrag unit shortly to be standardized on S2.2 Lotus Elites and Eclats, but it was very

Apart from the roll-cage inside the passenger compartment and the tailgate spoiler, this Talbot Horizon looks relatively normal . . .

. . . but under the skin there was a mid-mounted Esprit Turbo engine and Citroen-type transmission. It was Coventry's first thoughts on the theme of a 200-off Group B rally car for the mid-1980s, now overtaken by the Peugeot-designed Type 205 rally car. Only one example was built.

Among their many engineering contract activities, Lotus also found time to build this mid-engined rally prototype for Citroen. The basic car was Visa, but behind the seats there was a 2.5-litre Citroen Reflex engine of about 220bhp. One day, perhaps, Citroen might put this sort of rally car into limited production.

strong indeed, and could be modified in many ways to make it ideal for rallying in all conditions. Fifth gear in the road car application was a geared-up overdrive, and as a result the car was almost exactly as fast in fourth as in fifth gear. *Autocar's* testers recorded 121mph, with 0-60mph in 7.4 seconds, and a standing quarter-mile time of 15.6 seconds.

Incidentally, although there was no external evidence of a Lotus involvement in the Jensen-Healey, on the Talbot Sunbeam-Lotus not only was the name 'Lotus' in the car's title, but the famous Lotus 'ACBC' roundels were applied as transfers to the side of the bodyshells, ahead of the doors.

Lotus, in fact, were much more closely involved in the Sunbeam-Lotus project than they had ever been with the Jensen-Healey. Not only did they carry out a whirlwind development and proving exercise on behalf of the Coventry-based Engineering Division of Talbot (*nee* Chrysler), but they were also responsible for part-assembly of all the production cars.

Because of the proposed number of Sunbeam-Lotus cars to be built, there was insufficient space for all the work to be done at

Hethel. Accordingly, although the engines were machined, assembled and checked out at Hethel, car assembly was completed at another building (already owned by Lotus) on Ludham airfield, which is about 10 miles north-east of Norwich and nearly 20 miles from Hethel, in the heart of the Norfolk Broads area.

About 16 Lotus staff were drafted to Ludham, where pre-production began in March 1979 and continued to May 1981. Cars were built up to what I call the 'rolling chassis' stage at the Linwood factory (a few miles west of Glasgow, where all other Sunbeam hatchbacks were being built) and then transported to Ludham, where the Lotus staff not only mated Type 911 engines to German ZF gearboxes, but fitted these to the cars, along with larger-capacity water radiators and modifications to the transmission tunnel. The completed cars were then sent back to the factory in Coventry for final checking and inspection, before being delivered to the dealers.

Sales of the Sunbeam-Lotus began in the summer of 1979, and there were stocks in hand when the last cars were assembled in 1981. Talbot, like many other car makers before them, had over-estimated the demand for what was, after all, an homologation special, and total production, in fact, was only 1,150 right-hand-drive and 1,148 left-hand-drive cars, which made up a total of 2,298 in all — half of the intended sanction. Most were black, though the last few hundred were an attractive shade of blue, and it is worth recalling that no fewer than 30 examples were supplied to British police forces as well!

After Talbot withdrew from works rallying with these cars, sales virtually stopped, such that the last 150 examples were converted in 1983 to a super-luxury interior specification by Ladbroke Avon Coachworks, in Warwickshire. Assembly had stopped when the entire Talbot Sunbeam range was dropped and the Linwood factory was closed down.

The Sunbeam-Lotus was a very successful works rally car, even though it had a tentative and unlucky start. In 1979, Tony Pond was hired to drive the factory-built machines, but achieved very little, in spite of leading the Scottish and Manx rallies and holding third place on the Lombard-RAC until the last night of the event, when he crashed and had to retire.

Pond was no longer a team member in 1980, but Henri Toivonen and Guy Frequelin (Finnish and French, respectively) made up a two-car driving team. There was a gradual build-up of success, which culminated in Toivonen winning the prestigious Lombard-RAC rally outright, with two other Sunbeam-Lotuses (Frequelin and Russell Brookes) in third and fourth places.

The truly memorable season, however, unfolded in 1981

In 1976, Vauxhall produced and homologated the Chevette HS, equipped with their own 2.3-litre engine bottom end, to which a complete Lotus 16-valve Type 907 head, valve gear and carburation had been grafted. It won its first international rally in mid-1977.

when the Talbot factory team, using a mere six cars, tackled the entire World Rally Championship series. Although they won just one event (Guy Frequelin finished first in the Argentinian Codasur event), they also took second place on five more occasions (Monte Carlo, Portugal, Corsica, Brazil and San Remo), which was sufficient for them to win the Championship for Makes. Guy Frequelin himself was second in the Driver's series, behind Ari Vatanen (who used Ford Escorts throughout the year).

At the end of that season, Talbot withdrew from World Championship events, while the parent company, Peugeot, began the design of a new four-wheel-drive mid-engined car for 1983 and beyond. In the meantime, however, Des O'Dell and Lotus had co-operated in the building of a mid-engined Talbot Horizon prototype (where the engine was placed behind the front seats, driving the rear wheels only). This might, indeed, have become Talbot's new Group B rally car if the arrival of the Audi Quattro had not convinced most rival manufacturers that they, too, would need four-wheel-drive in the future. But wouldn't a turbocharged, mid-engined, Horizon look-alike have been exciting?

Finally, I should also mention Vauxhall's attempts to get on terms with Ford in the world of international rallying, and the way that Lotus were indirectly involved. Vauxhall first used the Magnum Coupes, and then progressed to Chevette HS and HSR models.

Dealer Team Vauxhall began by using Magnum Coupes fitted with the conventional single-cam iron-block 2,279cc Vauxhall engine. Next, however, they spotted a new regulation which allowed the use of an alternative cylinder head in competitions if they could guarantee that 100 kits had been sold for conversion purposes.

No-one now believes that anything like 100 such heads were ever supplied, but somehow Vauxhall achieved recognition and were able to go rallying with Magnums fitted with Lotus Type 907 cylinder heads, camshafts and carburettors mated to the original Vauxhall cast-iron cylinder blocks. Suddenly, it was 1968 all over again.

The Magnums were never very successful because they were too bulky and had unsatisfactory traction and handling, but the Chevette HS which followed was a much more competitive and serious project.

DTV persuaded Vauxhall that the only way to match and eventually beat the all-conquering Escorts was to produce the Chevette HS, for which 400 examples had to be built to secure Group 4 homologation. The HS models, effectively, were mainstream Chevette hatchbacks with the 2.3-litre slant-four Vauxhall engine and a *Vauxhall*-designed 16-valve cylinder head, allied to a stronger gearbox, and it was this specification which was planned to go into limited production.

The Chevette HS rally cars used Lotus 16-valve heads and carburation until the spring of 1978, when homologation was rescinded. To give clearance for the left-hand-drive steering column (for Pentti Airikkala's cars) the engine was installed at 35 degrees, rather than 45 degrees to the vertical. To disguise the head's parentage, the cars had 'Blydenstein' (after the company who prepared them) on the camshaft covers.

Chevette HS production cars which went on sale in 1978 had Vauxhall's own 16-valve cylinder head, an entirely different casting from the Lotus unit, as this engine bay shot makes clear, for the included angle between valves was different and the camshaft covers were at a different angle, too.

This is what the Chevette HS road car looked like — some of these cars may now have Lotus engines fitted, as Vauxhall parts supplies have long since run out.

Somehow, though, the Chevette HS came to be homologated in November 1976 on the strength of a single car — *the* prototype. This was well before production cars could possibly be built, and it was fitted with the Lotus Type 907 cylinder head! In this form it was easily capable of developing 240bhp, and within six months the Chevette HS had started to win British international events.

Soon there was something of a rumpus in the rallying world, not only because the Chevette had been homologated on very flimsy evidence indeed, but because it was so clearly meant to drive a great wedge into the spirit of rallying regulations.

The Chevette HS production car was not actually put on sale until April 1978 (16 months *after* the car had originally been homologated), when it was seen to have the Vauxhall, rather than the Lotus, cylinder head, the two light-alloy castings being entirely different. Predictably, therefore, there was a further sporting storm, the result being that the authorities temporarily rescinded the car's homologation, only being persuaded to restore it when the Vauxhall cylinder head and other proper production details had been standardized in the paperwork.

Chevettes with the Lotus-Vauxhall engine had always been fast, reliable and competitive, and certainly this was one of the factors which inspired Chrysler's Des O'Dell to produce a similar car for his own use. Incidentally, all credit to Vauxhall's engineers for producing a cylinder head which was eventually persuaded to liberate as much power as the race-proved Lotus head had always done, and to DTV's Bill Blydenstein for persisting against all the odds. The Vauxhall head, by the way, had its lines of valves opposed at an included angle of 31 degrees, compared with 38 degrees in the Lotus head.

CHAPTER 10

The De Lorean connection

Involvement in a lost cause

Mention of the ill-fated De Lorean project must be made in this book for two important reasons. One is that Lotus engineers were responsible for most of the design and development work on the car which went into production in Belfast's Dunmurry factory, and the other is that there were many close technical similarities in the chassis layout of the rear-engined De Lorean and the mid-engined Lotus Esprit. This is certainly not the place; however, to go into all the sordid commercial details surrounding the De Lorean company (which have already been published in several quarters), but merely to outline how Lotus came to be involved in the project and the part they played.

John Zachary De Lorean had been one of General Motors' most publicity-conscious 'young lions' in the 1960s and early 1970s. However, he abruptly resigned from a very senior corporate position in 1973, in circumstances which have never properly been explained, and within a year he had started to think about a new car design of his own. The De Lorean Motor Company was founded in 1974, by which time the concept of a rear-engined (*not* mid-engined, please note) two-seater coupe had already been dreamed up. It was to have stainless-steel skin panels, but a structure which mainly consisted of composite materials some way removed from simple glass-fibre; right from the start, too, it was always scheduled to have lift-up gull-wing doors. Only two production sports cars in the world — the Mercedes-Benz 300SL of the 1950s and the Bricklin SV-1 of the 1970s — had ever had such doors and neither car had sold in large numbers. At the end of 1974, De Lorean had picked Giorgetto Giugiaro and Ital Design to shape his dream car, and perhaps it was at this point that his first links, however tenuous and unconscious, were made with Lotus, for the talented Italian had just finalized the styling of the Esprit.

The first prototype, complete with a transversely-mounted Citroen CX four-cylinder engine and transmission, was completed in 1976, but it was found to be seriously underpowered. The second prototype of 1977 retained the same basic Ital Design body style and structure, but was equipped with the single-overhead-camshaft 90-degree V6 Renault 30 engine (of 2.66 litres — the PRV unit also used by Peugeot and Renault), and the transmission as also fitted to the Renault 30. In the Renault installation, incidentally, the engine was ahead of the final drive and the transmission behind it, driving the front wheels, whereas in the De Lorean the engine was behind the final drive and the transmission in front of it; to ensure correct operation in the De Lorean it was essential for Renault to flip over the crownwheel-and-pinion set, like the Alpine-Renault A310 V6 installation.

The project had already been dragging on for more than four years before De Lorean found anywhere to build production cars, and the state of the Renault-engined prototype could best be described as 'elementary'. The original scheme had been to use a multi-section Elastic Reservoir Moulding (ERM) plastics monocoque, in which 0.5in thick sheets of open-cell urethane foam were sandwiched between sheets of glass-fibre (and then moulded into shape under pressure in simple press tools). There were front and rear steel subframes, to support suspension, engine and transmission components, all bolted up to the plastics shell. However, even before the second prototype had been built, the ERM concept had been abandoned for the time being and pure

The ill-fated De Lorean coupe, on which Lotus development engineers did such a magnificent job between 1978 and 1980. The company's failure was certainly nothing to do with Lotus.

glass-fibre was used in its place. (The very first designer to use a glass-fibre monocoque was Colin Chapman, for the original Elite of 1957.)

In 1978, John De Lorean's three major problems were to raise finance to have the car put into production, to find a production site, and to have the design refined and finalized. It is now a matter of history that he nearly settled on a site in Puerto Rico, that a site near Shannon Airport in the Republic of Ireland was also considered, but that he eventually persuaded the British Government to lend and grant many millions of pounds for the sports coupe to be built in a brand new factory at Dunmurry, just south of Belfast, in Northern Ireland.

De Lorean first invited Lotus to have a look at the car during the summer of 1978, the result being that Colin Chapman and Mike Kimberley flew out to see the second prototype in Phoenix, Arizona. They have since been quoted as thinking that the car was 'abominable' at that time, and that De Lorean's development chief, Bill Collins, agreed with them . . .

Even so, although British Government finance for the project was agreed and made public in August 1978, Lotus were not contracted to develop the car until November of that year. For three months John De Lorean had been shopping around in Europe, particularly at Porsche, who had wanted a great deal of money and up to four years to do the job. Consequently, when Lotus agreed to do the same thing for less, and in a mere 18 months, they were signed up.

It was a very demanding contract, as Mike Kimberley recalls: 'We started with only a package — a style — and we had to provide engineering facilities — design, engineering development and prototype build. We did it under the guidance of Chuck Bennington, their Managing Director, who spent four days out of every seven at Hethel. We were given 18 months to do the job, a pace which no other company in Europe could have achieved.'

The fact that the finance for this business came to Lotus via a Panama-registered company called General Products Development Services Inc (GPD), and not direct from De

Dramatis personae — John De Lorean (centre), Mike Kimberley (right) and Lotus engineering chief Colin Spooner in discussion over the new De Lorean project.

Lorean, was a puzzling financial wrinkle which has no part of this technical story. There was no doubt, however, that the money was for real, and available. De Lorean established an engineering and purchasing facility in Coventry, and also drafted a small team into Hethel and Ketteringham Hall. Lotus allocated the largest building on the site — a vast hangar which had to be refurbished — for this, their largest-yet consulting job. Lotus demanded, and got, virtually a free hand to redesign the car as their engineering judgment dictated. It was clear, right at the start, that the prototype's unique construction was going to be controversial — as Jeffrey Daniels of *Autocar* pointed out in his technical analysis of October 1977: '. . . instead of a plastic body on a steel frame, we see in effect a steel body on a plastic frame . . .'.

Lotus were most unhappy about it all, not merely because the prototype's roadholding and general rigidity were not helped by the big cut-outs in the shell dictated by the gull-wing doors, but also beause of the safety limitations. Their own vast experience of both glass-fibre-based bodies and backbone chassis-frames led them to surmise that in its original guise the De Lorean would fare very badly indeed in a barrier crash test. Very shortly Grumman (the US aerospace concern) were invited in by De Lorean to analyse the structure on their most sophisticated computers; they did so and predicted that the rear-mounted engine and gearbox would catch up with the occupants in the front footwells in a 26mph crash test!

Before the De Lorean was ready to go into production it had virtually become a rear-engined (Renault-engined) Lotus, with a familiar type of backbone frame and independent suspension inside the Ital Design shape. Even the styling was altered, for in 1979, in mid-contract, De Lorean decided that it had been around

The bare bones of an early De Lorean development chassis-frame, showing clearly how its design philosophy was very much that of the modern-generation Lotus cars.

A display example of the De Lorean DMC12's production chassis, showing how the fuel tank sits between the front forks of the backbone, and the engine is hung out at the back. In many ways, including the wishbone front suspension, independent rear suspension layout and the use of Goodyear NCT tyres, the De Lorean is close to the Esprit — but Colin Chapman would never have considered using a rear-engined layout.

The suspension geometry looks rather like that of the Esprit S3/Turbo cars, but the car is the De Lorean, with the rear-end dominated by the big 90-degrees 2.85-litre PRV V6 engine.

too long and needed to be freshened up before going on sale, and he asked Ital Design to facelift everything. As Lotus were already on such a tight schedule that they had finalized the skin contours well before the rest of the car was fixed, it meant that new skins and window shapes and cut-outs had to be redrawn, and that everything abutting those profiles — which meant the composite bodyshell, trim panels, glass and many other details — had to be modified. The change, Mike Kimberley says, came 10 months into the 18-month contract and caused a considerable delay, which stretched the job, in the end, to 25 months. The project, which was absorbing well over half of Lotus' entire strength when at its peak, should have been finished in May 1980, but was eventually wound up at the end of the year. As I have already pointed out, the sheer size of this project inevitably meant that there was delay to the development and production of Lotus' new

models for the 1980s, although this leeway has now largely been made up.

The De Lorean sports coupe went on sale during 1981, but the company collapsed into bankruptcy in 1982, and this meant that the car was only ever marketed in the United States. In Federal form its PRV V6 engine had been enlarged to 2,849cc (as in the latest Volvo 760GLE saloon, for instance) and it produced up to 130bhp. The unladen weight was only 2,840lb, which reflected great credit on the Lotus design team and their experience with such structures. It was not, however, anything like as quick as its looks suggested it should have been. *Road & Track's* authoritative road test showed that the top speed was a mere 109mph (in fifth *or* fourth gear), that 0-60mph acceleration took a rather pedestrian 10.5 seconds, and that 0-100mph needed no less than 40 seconds and a lot of straight highway. All this helped to give the car its

The front suspension of the De Lorean sports car had clear historical links with that of the Esprit, and it had the same sort of job to do. The fuel tank is low down between the front arms of the backbone frame.

'gutless' reputation, right from the start. Day-to-day fuel consumption was quoted as 19mpg (US gallons)/22.8mpg (Imperial gallons).

Apart from the De Lorean's rather limited performance, there was also the question of its handling. John DeLorean was once quoted as saying that the car handled better than most other sports cars and that the rear-engined layout had to be right, for that was how Porsche built the 911. Since no British journalist was allowed to test the car while it was still in production, it was not easy to find out the truth of the matter.

However, my colleagues on *Autocar* got their hands on a 'clearance sale' example at the end of 1982, and Michael Scarlett had some interesting observations to make, the most penetrating of which was: 'Later, doubts returned with the uneasy, unfamiliarly spooky feeling of a well-overhung engine behind. No matter how good the suspension or the Lotus development engineer, you can't disguise the effects of a high rear-based polar moment, whose beginnings lead inexorably to earthier moments.'

Everyone agreed that Lotus engineers had done a fine job, starting from a very difficult imposed design layout. The backbone chassis-frame, so like that of the Esprit in general layout, was built for De Lorean by GKN in the West Midlands, and was coated with fusion-bonded epoxy resin for anti-corrosion protection. All the running gear was neatly packaged around it, not only with the engine and transmission in the extreme tail, but with the fuel tank in the nose, between the front forks of the

De Loreans in series production at the Dunmurry plant, south of Belfast, early in 1981, when hopes were high and up to 40 cars a day were being built.

backbone. Front suspension (by unequal-length wishbones, coil springs and an anti-roll bar, linked to rack-and-pinion steering without power assistance), and rear suspension (by upper and lower links, a long fabricated semi-trailing arm and coil spring/damper units) were both like the latest Esprit installation.

The rear engine ensured that a majority of weight would be over the back wheels (the actual bias was 35/65 per cent front-to-rear), and to tame this Lotus had provided 195/60HR-14in tyres on 6in rims at the front, but 235/60HR-15in tyres on 8in rims at the rear. The philosophy which went so far to making the Esprit one of the best handling cars in the world had thoroughly been applied to the De Lorean project.

Even so, the result was not entirely satisfactory. Michael Scarlett summed it all up very well with this comment: 'If there were European DMC 12s on sale, I can't see why it should have succeeded one whit more easily here than it did in the easier, sometimes more gullible, American sports car market. Regardless of John DeLorean's good and bad points, I think now, as I have always thought, simply that it was silly to build and try to sell a rear-engined sports car.'

In many respects, the De Lorean was even made in the same way as the modern Lotus models. The bodyshell was built from two major mouldings by the patented Lotus VARI resin-injection method. John De Lorean had been thinking big, for there were half-a-dozen sets of mould tools — at £25,000-£30,000 each — whose capacity was way above any volume that even the super-optimistic De Lorean had ever forecast.

The failure, and most of the facts, of the De Lorean business is now well known. The car, indeed, had a short and very turbulent life. Pilot production began in December 1980 (as soon as Lotus' job was finished) and the first real production car rolled out on January 21, 1981. The original shipment was made to the USA in June 1981, at which point 40 cars a day were built. This rate was doubled to 80 a day in November, but by this time the car's Stateside reputation was already in trouble. Sales slumped, stocks of unsold cars piled up in both Belfast and North America, and the Receivers, Cork Gully, were appointed in February 1982. Production continued, slowly and haltingly, for some months, but by October it was all over.

The basic reason was not only that the car, as a driving machine, was disappointing, but that it was also far too expensive at $25,000. I simply do not understand how John De Lorean, with a lifetime of experience in that most down-to-earth corporation, General Motors, could ever have expected to sell 25,000 expensive De Loreans a year — taking the Chevrolet Corvette head-on — when all the evidence suggested that the *total* US market for imported exotica was below this level. His factory was rigged for this sort of production level — which equated to up to 600 cars a week — as a result of which the financial break-even point was 10,000 cars a year. The reason for the company's bankruptcy, therefore, can be spelt out in one sentence — in 23 months a mere 8,000 cars were built and at the end of the day a proportion of these cars were still unsold.

Lotus, fortunately, were paid for most of their work before the various and ever-evolving De Lorean scandals broke out. By that time the car story was at an end. As for the financial story, that is one which could run, and run, for years.

'The Iron Lady' — Mrs Margaret Thatcher, the Prime Minister — talking to Colin Chapman and Mike Kimberley from the driving seat of a Lotus Esprit.

They say that Colin Chapman not only approved the design of the factory and office buildings at Hethel, but also supervized the layout of the attractive grounds as well — he was never a man to let such detail slip by without comment.

An overhead view of Hethel, with the test track slipping across the picture in front of the buildings. The office complex is in the centre, with the machine shop behind it, and the secret development shops are to the left. The main engine, chassis and final assembly areas are to the right, and the bodyshell plant (closed to all but favoured visitors) is on the extreme right. The De Lorean 'hangar' is out of shot, further to the right, and the public road to the east of the site is near the top of the picture.

APPENDIX A
Technical specifications

As I have already made clear in the main text of this book, there are two basically different families of cars to be considered. The front-engined chassis of 1974 to date covers the Elite, Eclat and Excel models, while the mid-engined chassis of 1976 to date covers the Esprit and the Esprit Turbo. The technical information provided below has been grouped accordingly, to make it easier to understand.

The Elite model had the front-engined chassis, along with the hatchback style of coupe bodywork.

The Eclat and Excel models had the front-engined chassis, along with a fastback style of coupe bodywork, the front of which was identical to that of the Elite.

The Esprit had the entirely different mid-engined chassis, with Giugiaro-styled two-seater coupe bodywork.

No convertible version of any of these cars has ever been offered for sale.

Elite S1 — produced 1974 to 1980

Engine: 4-cyl, twin overhead camshaft, 95.28 × 69.24mm, 1,973cc, CR 9.5:1, 2 twin-choke Dellorto DHLA carbs. Original cars 155bhp (DIN) at 6,500rpm; maximum torque 135lb/ft at 5,000rpm. From early production onwards, 160bhp (DIN) at 6,200rpm. Maximum torque 140lb/ft at 4,900rpm.

Transmission: 5-speed all-synchromesh manual gearbox. Final-drive ratio 3.73:1 on first cars, then optional to 4.1:1 ratio. Overall gear ratios (4.1:1 final-drive) 3.29, 4.1, 5.62, 8.28, 13.12, reverse 14.19:1. (3.73:1 final-drive) 3.00, 3.73, 5.11, 7.53, 11.94, reverse 12.91:1. 20.8mph/1,000rpm in top gear (4.1:1 final-drive), or 22.9mph/1,000rpm in top gear (3.73:1 final-drive).

Optional on Elite 504 only, from autumn 1975, Borg-Warner 3-speed automatic transmission. Final-drive ratio 3.73:1. Overall gear ratios 3.73, 5.41, 8.91, reverse 7.80:1. 18.9mph/1,000rpm in top gear.

Suspension and brakes: Ifs, coil springs, wishbones, anti-roll bar and telescopic dampers; irs, coil springs, lower wishbones, fixed-length drive-shafts and telescopic dampers. Rack-and-pinion steering (with power assistance on Type 503 and 504 models). 10.4in front discs brakes, 9 × 2¼in rear drum brakes, with vacuum servo assistance. 205/60VR—14in tyres on 7in rim cast-alloy wheels.

Dimensions: Wheelbase 8ft 1.8in; front track 4ft 10.5in; rear track 4ft 11in. Length 14ft 7.5in; width 5ft 11.5in; height 3ft 11.5in. Unladen weight 2,440lb, rising to 2,550lb with air conditioning and power-assisted steering. Maximum payload 890lb.

Original price: (May 1974) Elite 501, £4,568 (basic), £5,445 including taxes; 502, £4,915 (basic), £5,857 including taxes.

Differences for USA and Japanese markets:
Engine: CR 8.4:1, 2 Zenith-Stromberg CD single-choke carbs. 140bhp (DIN) at 6,500rpm. Maximum torque 130lb/ft at 5,000rpm.

Elite S2.2 — produced 1980 to date

Basic specification as for Elite S1, except for:
Engine: 95.28 × 76.2mm, 2,174cc, CR 9.4:1. 160bhp (DIN) at 6,500rpm. Maximum torque 160lb/ft at 5,000rpm.

Transmission: Getrag 5-speed all-synchromesh manual gearbox specified in place of Lotus (BL-geared) box. Standard final-drive ratio 4.1:1, optional 3.73:1, and 3.73:1 with automatic transmission. Overall gear ratios (4.1:1 final-drive) 3.33, 4.1, 5.70, 7.91, 12.14, reverse 15.19:1. (3.73:1 final-drive) 3.03, 3.73, 5.18, 7.20, 11.04, reverse 13.82:1. 21.14mph/1,000rpm in top gear (4.1:1 final-drive) or 23.3mph/1,000rpm in top gear (3.73:1 final-drive).

Suspension and brakes: Power-assisted steering optional (only one model).

Dimensions: Unladen weight 2,645lb. Maximum payload 860lb.

Original price: (May 1980) £16,142 (total), without power-assisted steering or air conditioning.

Eclat S1 — produced 1975 to 1980

Basic specification as for Elite S1, except for:
Transmission: 4-speed all-synchromesh (Ford Granada/Capri) manual gearbox on Type 520 derivative — Types 521/522/523 having normal Lotus 5-speed gearbox. Final-drive ratio 3.73:1. Overall gear ratios (4-speed gearbox) 3.73, 5.26, 7.27, 11.79, reverse 12.50:1. 17.9mph/1,000rpm in top gear (4-speed transmission), 22.9mph/1,000rpm in top gear (5-speed transmission). Automatic transmission available on Type 524 from spring 1976.

Suspension and brakes: On Type 520 only, 185/70HR—13in tyres on 5.5in rim pressed-steel wheels. Other derivatives as Elite S1.

Dimensions: Basically as Elite, through Type 523 approximately 100lb lighter than Type 503 Elite.

Original price: (October 1975) Eclat Type 520 £5,729 (total, including taxes).

Eclat Sprint — produced 1977
Mechanically as Eclat S1 Type 520 and 521, except for cosmetic changes and 5.5in rim alloy road wheels instead of steel wheels on Type 520, and 4.1:1 final-drive ratio on 5-speed transmission Type 521.
Original price: (February 1977) Type 520 Sprint £7,842 (total), and Type 521 Sprint £8,372, compared with £7,544 and £8,074 for existing Eclat models.

Eclat S2.2 — produced 1980 to 1982
Basic specification as for Eclat S1, with engine and transmission of Elite S2.2, except for:
Transmission: 4-speed gearbox no longer available.
Suspension and brakes: Pressed-steel wheels and 185-section tyres no longer available.
Original price: (May 1980) £15,842 (total).

Eclat S2.2 Riviera — produced 1981 and 1982
Limited-edition Eclat S2.2, mechanically unchanged, but with lift-out roof panel, rear spoiler and other distinctive styling touches.
Original price: (October 1981) £14,857 (total).

Excel — produced 1982 to date
Extensively re-engineered Eclat, still with same basic chassis, but different style, rear suspension and using Toyota transmission and brake components.
Engine: As Elite/Eclat S2.2.
Transmission: 5-speed all-synchromesh Toyota manual gearbox. Final-drive ratio 4.1:1. Overall gear ratios 3.20, 4.1, 4.96, 7.75, 13.49, reverse 15.45:1. 21.2mph/1,000rpm in top gear. Automatic transmission not available.
Suspension: Ifs as Eclat S2.2; irs, coil springs, lower wishbones, upper links, telescopic dampers. Rack-and-pinion steering (optional power assistance). 10.16in front disc brakes, 10.47in rear disc brakes, with vacuum servo assistance. 205/60VR—14in tyres on 7in rim cast-alloy wheels.
Dimensions: Wheelbase 8ft 1.8in; front track 4ft 9.5in; rear track 4ft 9.5in. Length 14ft 4.3in; width 5ft 11.5in; height 3ft 11.5in. Unladen weight 2,503lb; maximum payload 890lb.
Original price: (October 1982) £13,787 (total).

Esprit S1 — produced 1976 to 1978
Engine: 4-cyl, twin overhead camshaft, 95.28 × 69.24mm, 1,973cc, CR 9.5:1, 2 twin-choke Dellorto DHLA carbs. 160bhp (DIN) at 6,200rpm. Maximum torque 140lb/ft at 4,900rpm.
Transmission: 5-speed all-synchromesh Citroen SM/Maserati Merak-type manual gearbox, in unit with engine and final-drive. Final-drive ratio 4.375:1. Overall gear ratios 3.33, 4.24, 5.77, 8.49, 12.77, reverse 15.14:1. 21.85mph/1,000rpm in top gear.

Suspension and brakes: Ifs, coil springs, wishbones, anti-roll bar and telescopic dampers; irs, coil springs, lower wishbone/semi-trailing arms, fixed-length drive-shafts and telescopic dampers. Rack-and-pinion steering, no power assistance. 9.7in front disc brakes, 10.6in rear disc brakes, with vacuum servo assistance. 205/60HR—14in front tyres on 6in rim cast-alloy wheels, with 205/70HR—14in rear tyres on 7in rim cast-alloy wheels.
Dimensions: Wheelbase 8ft 0in; front track 4ft 11.5in; rear track 4ft 11.5in. Length 13ft 9in; width 6ft 1.25in; height 3ft 7.7in. Unladen weight 2,218lb; maximum payload 500lb.
Original price: (July 1976) £6,738 (basic), £7,883 including taxes.
Differences for USA and Japanese markets:
Engine: CR 8.4:1. 2 Zenith-Stromberg CD single-choke carbs. 140bhp (DIN) at 6,500rpm. Maximum torque 130lb/ft at 5,000rpm.
Dimensions: Length 13ft 11.7in. Unladen weight 2,350lb.

Esprit S2 — produced 1978 to 1980
Specification as for Esprit S1, except for:
Suspension and brakes: Front wheels had 7in rim width, rear wheels 7.5in rim width, and special spare wheels had 185/70HR—13in tyre and 5.5in rim width.
Dimensions: Unladen weight 2,334lb.
Original price: (August 1978) £11,124 (total).

Esprit S2.2 — produced 1980 and 1981
Specification as for Esprit S2, except for:
Engine: 95.28 × 76.2mm, 2,174cc, CR 9.4:1. 160bhp (DIN) at 6,500rpm. Maximum torque 160lb/ft at 5,000rpm.
Original price: (May 1980) £14,951 (total).

Esprit S3 — produced 1981 to date
Specification as for Esprit S2.2, except for:
Suspension and brakes: Ifs as before; irs by coil springs, lower wishbones/semi-trailing arms, upper links and telescopic dampers. 10.5in front disc brakes, 10.8in rear disc brakes. Basic wheel/tyre equipment as before. Optional: 195/60VR—15in front tyres on 7in rim alloy wheels, with 235/60VR—15in rear tyres on 8in rim alloy wheels; special spare wheel with 175/70SR—14in tyre; 22.7mph/1,000rpm in top gear.
Dimensions: With optional wheels/tyres, front track 5ft 0.5in; rear track 5ft 1.2in. Unladen weight 2,352lb.
Original price: (April 1981) £13,461 (total).

Esprit Turbo — produced 1980 to date
Basic layout as for Esprit S3, except for:
Engine: 4-cyl, twin overhead camshaft, 95.28 × 76.2mm, 2,174cc, CR 7.5:1, 2 twin-choke Dellorto DHLA carbs and Garrett AiResearch T3

turbocharger. 210bhp (DIN) at 6,000rpm. Maximum torque 200lb/ft at 4,000rpm.
Transmission: As S3, except 22.7mph/1,000rpm in top gear.
Suspension and brakes: As S3, but 15in wheel and tyre equipment standard.

Dimensions: Unladen weight 2,653lb; maximum payload 466lb.
Original price: (February 1980) £20,950 (total) in Essex limited-edition form. (April 1981) £16,982 (total) in normal production form.
Differences for USA and Japanese markets, cars produced from 1983: 205bhp (SAE) at 6,000-6,500rpm.

APPENDIX B
Chassis number sequences

In the good old days, Before Legislation, and Before Type Approval, identifying a car was easy enough. A sequence of chassis numbers usually started at . . 001 with the first car of all, and continued, number for number, until the model was withdrawn. But all that has changed.

Manufacturers like Lotus now not only use different numbering sequences for cars sent to different markets, but they also have to fall in line with the very complex and lengthy VIN (Vehicle Identification Number) system now imposed on car makers throughout the European Economic Community.

Nevertheless, there are still ways of 'picking' one modern Lotus from another. The factory have very kindly provided a table, containing information which is reproduced below, which should allow the origin of any Elite, Eclat, Excel and Esprit to be ascertained with ease. Buyers of new Lotus cars know what type of cars they had ordered, but those buying them at second, or third hand may need to recheck a claimed history.

Up to the end of 1979, the VIN number was stamped on a plate fixed to the right-hand wheelarch in the engine bay, and from 1980 (a legal requirement), there was also a plate mounted on the facia crash-roll, which had to be visible through the windscreen from outside.

From 1980 to date, the numbers are extremely complex, for no fewer than 17 characters — letters or numbers — are involved. Up to the end of 1979, however, the number was not only shorter, but easier to decipher. Here is an example:

7501 0404 A

The first two numbers (75 in this case) indicate the calendar year in which the car was built. The second two numbers (01) indicate the month. The final numbers are the actual chassis number. The final letter indicated the market for which the car was built. For the UK, the letter for an Elite was 'A', for an Eclat 'D' and for an Esprit 'G'. For the USA, the Elite letter was 'B', the Eclat letter 'E' and for the Esprit 'H', at first, but once different specifications were required for California alone, things became more complex. It is hardly the task of this book to list all sub-derivatives delineated in factory literature.

Identification *by number* of major models is, however, as follows:

First and last chassis numbers (First and last dates built)

Model	UK market	USA/Federal/Japan (including California before 1979 model)	California only	Rest of the World
Elite S1	0001A - 1636A (Mar 1974 - Nov 1979	0001B - 0516B (May 1974 - Feb 1981)	—	0001C - 0236C (Apr 1974 - Oct 1979)
— from 1979. model	—	0100K - 0144K (Dec 1978 - Mar 1980)	0100L - 0142L (Dec 1978 - Mar 1980)	—
Elite S2.2	1637A - 1757 (Apr 1980 - Jan 1983)	—	—	0237C - 0243 (Jul 1980 - Jan 1982
Eclat S1	0100D - 0956D (Oct 1975 - Dec 1979)	0100E - 0397E (Nov 1975 - Feb 1981)	—	0100F - 0205F (Dec 1975 - Oct 1979)
— from 1979 model	—	0100P - 0148P (Aug 1978 - Aug 1980)	0100U - 0150U (Oct 1978 - Jul 1980)	—

Model	UK market	USA/Federal/Japan (including California before 1979 model)	California only	Rest of the World
Eclat S2.2	957 - 1143 (Apr 1980 - July 1982)	—	—	0206 - 0232 (Sep 1980 - Jul 1982)
Excel	First No: 1144 (Oct 1982)	—	—	First No: 0233 (Sep 1982)
Esprit S1	0100G - 0312G (May 1976 - Dec 1977)	0100H - 0566H (Dec 1976 - Dec 1977)	—	0100J - 0136J (Jan 1977 - Dec 1977)
Esprit S2	0313G - 0857G (Dec 1977 - Nov 1979)	0567H - 0863H (Dec 1977 - Jul 1978)	—	0137J - 0357J (Jan 1978 - Feb 1981)
— from 1979 model	—	0100S - 0259S (Sep 1978 - Feb 1980)	0100T - 0255T (Oct 1978 - Jan 1980)	—
Esprit S2.2	0861 - 0994 (Jan 1980 - Mar 1981)	—	—	0358 - 0361 (Mar 1981 - Mar 1981)
Esprit S3	First No: 0976 (Apr 1981)	—	—	First No: 0362 (Jun 1981)
Esprit Turbo	First No: 0900 (Aug 1980)	—	—	First No: 0300 (Sep 1980)
— USA all	—	First No: 0271 (Dec 1982)	—	—
— Canada	—	First No: 0260 (Jul 1981)	—	—
— Japan	—	First No: 0100 (Aug 1980)	—	—

Note: Production of Elite S2.2s had ceased by the beginning of 1983.
Production of redeveloped Federal Esprit Turbos began, in considerable numbers, in the winter of 1982/83.

APPENDIX C

Production and deliveries — 1974 to 1982

The new family of Lotus cars was much more complex, exclusive and expensive than the Elans and Europas which they replaced, and for that reason they could not possibly be expected to sell in similar quantities. Bear this in mind, therefore, when comparing the best production year of the Elite/Eclat/Esprit era, of 1,200 cars, with the 4,506 Elan/Europa models built in 1969.

Here are the facts and figures for the modern generation of Lotus products, complete to the end of the 1982 calendar year, along with statistics related to the Jensen-Healey and Talbot Sunbeam-Lotus projects:

Lotus annual production — 1968 to 1982

Calendar year	Elan/Europa production	Elite/Eclat/ Excel/Esprit production	Total production
1968	3,048	—	3,048
1969	4,506	—	4,506
1970	3,373	—	3,373
1971	2,682	—	2,682
1972	2,996	—	2,996
1973	2,822*	—	2,822
1974	760**	687	1,447
1975	56	479***	535
1976	—	935****	935
1977	—	1,070	1,070
1978	—	1,200	1,200
1979	—	1,031	1,031
1980	—	383	383
1981	—	345	345
1982	—	541	541

* Elan production ended in February 1973.
** Elan Plus 2 production ended in December 1974.
*** Eclat production began in the autumn of 1975.
**** Esprit production began in summer 1976.
Note: 1968 was the year in which Group Lotus was founded as a public company.

The next table shows the individual achievements of each different type of Lotus in much more detail. As far as possible, the model types and their sub-derivatives have been split up and the trends revealed are fascinating:

Model	Calendar year									Totals
	1974	1975	1976	1977	1978	1979	1980	1981	1982	
Elite S1	687	459	453	210	293	276	20	—	—	2,398
S2.2	—	—	—	—	—	—	105	13	14	132
Eclat S1	—	20	344	280	354	281	20	—	—	1,299
S2.2	—	—	—	—	—	—	101	31	91	223
Excel	—	—	—	—	—	—	—	—	71	71
Esprit S1	—	—	138	580	—	—	—	—	—	718
S2	—	—	—	—	553	474	18	15	—	1,060
S2.2	—	—	—	—	—	—	62	26	—	88
S3	—	—	—	—	—	—	—	144	160	304
Turbo	—	—	—	—	—	—	57	116	205	378
Totals	687	479	935	1,070	1,200	1,031	383	345	541	6,671

Notes:
Elite production declined considerably after 1979 as customer tastes changed and the merits of the very completely equipped Eclat S2.2 became more widely known. The Elite S2.2 has really been built only to special order since 1981.

Excel production got under way in the autumn of 1982 and the car was being built at the best possible rate by the beginning of 1983, when it was already selling faster than the last of the Eclat S2.2s.

Although the Esprit was first shown to the public in October 1975, the first deliveries were not made until June 1976.

The first 100 Esprit Turbos were decorated as 'Essex Commemorative' models, with distinctive colour schemes.

Home and export deliveries — year by year

This table shows how Lotus deliveries to North America boomed in the late 1970s, but fell rapidly away after the double change of distributing arrangements in 1979. Series production of new-type Federal Esprit Turbo models began early in 1983, and the first shipments were made in March/April 1983. Yet another Lotus importing concern has been established in the USA, and sales are expected to reach 350 in 1983 and up to 700 in 1986.

Total production breakdown:

Year	1974	1975	1976	1977	1978	1979	1980	1981	1982
Home Market	395	291	655	361	771	731	290	268	419
USA/Federal	42	144	190	633	336	164	53	17	3
Rest of World	250	44	90	76	93	136	40	60	119
Totals	687	479	935	1,070	1,200	1,031	383	345	541

Note: The short-lived US-market joint marketing deal with Rolls-Royce Motors was formalized in 1979, but abandoned in 1982. Far from helping sales of Lotus cars in the USA, the figures seem to indicate that the deal was a complete failure. USA exports have been relaunched in 1983.

Engine supplies to Jensen and Talbot

The 16-valve Type 907 2-litre engine was originally supplied to Jensen before it was offered in the Lotus Elite. The Jensen-Healey and its near-relative the Jensen GT were on sale from 1972 to 1976. During that time, a total of 10,453 Jensen-Healeys and 459 Jensen GTs — 10,912 cars in all — were built. Altogether 7,709 Jensen-Healeys were exported to the USA and 830 to other export markets.

As explained in the text, the Talbot Sunbeam-Lotus contract was more complex, with Lotus actually taking on assembly of engines to gearboxes, and engines/gearboxes to the cars themselves, at Ludham, near Norwich. Between March 1979, when pre-production began, and May 1981, when the last car was assembled, a total of 2,298 Sunbeam-Lotus cars were built. These used the original type of 2.2-litre engine.

APPENDIX D
How fast? How thirsty? How heavy?
Performance figures for the modern Lotus

When it came to compiling this section, I had no shortage of choice. Although Lotus rarely keep many demonstrator cars, they make sure that the small fleet is always very busy and every magazine tester fights for his chance to drive one of them.

However, when quoting performance figures, I like to compare like with like. Once again, in this series of *Collector's Guides,* I am grateful to my good friends on *Autocar,* not only for allowing me to quote their figures, but for having sampled almost every important derivative in the last decade! I have only needed to quote *Motor* in one instance — regarding the Elite S1 Type 504 with automatic transmission — and where appropriate I have also consulted *Road & Track,* of North America, for the performance of 'Federalized' Lotus models.

Elite, Eclat and Excel

It is, perhaps, significant that *Autocar* were offered an Elite S1 for test in the summer of 1974, but that this offer was withdrawn when Lotus themselves found their car to be not as fast as hoped. As a consequence, the specified final-drive ratio was altered (from 3.73:1 to 4.1:1 — see main text), and the car actually offered at the beginning of 1975 was better.

These were the capabilities of the front-engined cars tried:

	Elite S1 Type 503 1,973cc 160bhp (DIN)	Elite S1 Type 504 1,973cc 160bhp (DIN)	Elite S2.2 2,174cc 160bhp (DIN)	Eclat S1 Type 523 1,973cc 160bhp (DIN)	Excel 2,174cc 160bhp (DIN)
Mean maximum speed (mph)	124	119	127	129	130
Acceleration (sec)					
0-30mph	2.8	3.9	2.9	2.7	2.4
0-40mph	4.2	5.7	4.4	4.3	3.9
0-50mph	5.9	7.9	5.9	5.9	5.5
0-60mph	7.8	10.4	7.5	7.9	7.1
0-70mph	10.8	13.6	10.8	11.1	9.7
0-80mph	14.0	17.6	13.6	14.5	12.3
0-90mph	18.4	22.9	17.6	18.9	15.8
0-100mph	24.5	31.6	22.5	25.1	20.1
0-110mph	37.3	—	29.9	34.2	26.4
0-120mph	—	—	40.7	—	38.2
Standing ¼-mile (sec)	16.4	17.3	16.1	16.2	15.4
Top gear acceleration (sec)		(Kickdown — direct drive)			
20-40mph	—	3.7	—	—	12.1
30-50mph	15.4	4.2	11.9	13.1	11.4
40-60mph	14.4	5.5	10.8	12.1	9.3
50-70mph	13.7	6.4	9.2	12.3	9.1
60-80mph	15.4	8.2	10.3	14.1	9.8
70-90mph	17.8	11.2	12.4	16.4	10.0
80-100mph	20.7	15.6	13.2	18.4	11.2
Overall fuel consumption (mpg Imp)	20.9	19.1	20.6	20.7	19.5
Typical fuel consumption (mpg Imp)	25	22	23	23	22
Kerb weight (lb)	2,552	2,643	2,646	2,439	2,478
Original test published	Jan 1975	Aug 1978	Oct 1980	Jul 1977	Apr 1983

Notes:

There is no valid comparison between the 'top gear' capability of *Motor's* Elite 504 Automatic and *Autocar's* Elite Type 503; on the one hand, the automatic transmission car's figures were taken in 'Kickdown' (*ie,* with lower gears engaged up to about 70 or 80 mph), and in addition the overall gearing of the manual transmission car is significantly higher.

Perhaps, too, we should not draw too many conclusions between the different performance figures of the Elite and Eclat S1 cars, which are well within the 'scatter' due to variations in production engine outputs. It may be significant, however, that the Eclat had a higher top speed — subjectively, the aerodynamics of the fastback Eclat always look cleaner than those of the hatchback Elite, and the 5mph top speed difference seems to confirm this.

The performance of the latest Excel, however, is quite outstanding. On the assumption that the engine was merely a standard unit in top form, this must mean that Lotus' claim that the transmission losses have been reduced is vindicated — even though claims of a more favourable aerodynamic C_d factor are not proven. Even so, by comparison — say — with the Elite S2.2 of 1980, the Excel is better in all respects except fuel consumption.

Esprit and Esprit Turbo

A great deal of controversy still surrounds the true performance of the S1 Esprit, as *Autocar's* test car certainly produced a disappointing top speed and was not as accelerative as Lotus claimed it should have been. (*Motor's* test car — a different example — also had a disappointing top speed, and its standing-start figures are in any case suspect as the quarter-mile time is almost the same as that recorded by *Autocar* while the 0-80mph figure is 2.5 seconds quicker!).

Accordingly, we should look on the S2 as the representative example of 2-litre Esprit performance. No-one, by the way, is complaining about the pace of the S3, or the Turbo derivatives!

	Esprit S1 1,973cc 160bhp (DIN)	Esprit S2 1,973cc 160bhp (DIN)	Esprit S3 2,174cc 160bhp (DIN)	Esprit Turbo 2,174cc 210bhp (DIN)	Esprit S1 (USA) 1,973cc 140bhp (DIN)
Mean maximum speed (mph)	124*	135	134	148	120
Acceleration (sec)					
0-30mph	2.9	2.8	2.3	2.3	3.1
0-40mph	4.3	4.2	3.5	3.2	4.5
0-50mph	6.3	5.9	5.0	4.7	6.7
0-60mph	8.4	8.0	6.7	6.1	9.2
0-70mph	11.6	10.7	9.6	8.3	12.3
0-80mph	15.3	13.8	12.4	10.3	16.2
0-90mph	20.2	17.4	16.1	13.0	21.7
0-100mph	27.4	22.7	20.9	17.0	—
0-110mph	39.4	30.7	27.9	20.7	—
0-120mph	—	—	40.7	27.1	—
0-130mph	—	—	—	39.2	—
Standing ¼-mile (sec)	16.3	16.0	15.5	14.6	17.0
Top gear acceleration (sec)					
20-40mph	—	15.4	—	14.9	—
30-50mph	13.9	14.4	10.4	10.4	—
40-60mph	12.4	13.6	10.0	8.3	—
50-70mph	12.9	12.9	9.9	8.5	—
60-80mph	12.5	13.8	10.0	8.4	—
70-90mph	13.4	15.7	11.2	8.7	—
80-100mph	17.0	16.6	12.9	9.2	—
90-110mph	23.6	21.1	16.9	10.5	—
100-120mph	—	—	—	13.1	—
110-130mph	—	—	—	19.3	—
Overall fuel consumption (mpg Imp)	23.3	19.4	21.7	18.0	27.5**
Typical fuel consumption (mpg Imp)	26	21	24	20	—
Kerb weight (lb)	2,275	2,334	2,489	2,653	2,480
Original test published	Jan 1977	Jan 1979	Jun 1981	May 1981	Jul 1977

Notes:
* The test car could not exceed 124mph, when 138mph was claimed — and all the evidence points to a lack of top-end power, for acceleration at lower rpm is more closely related to that claimed by Lotus.

** This figure is quoted in US miles per gallon — and gives an Imperial equivalent of around 33, which is mind-bogglingly economical! The US open-road speed limits have a lot to answer for! *Road & Track*, who published this test, do not observe top-gear acceleration figures.